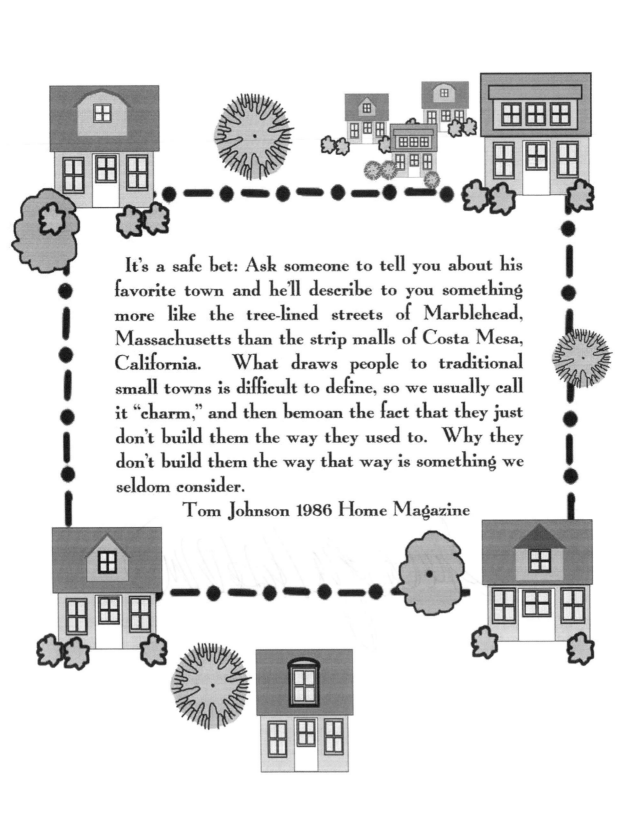

It's a safe bet: Ask someone to tell you about his favorite town and he'll describe to you something more like the tree-lined streets of Marblehead, Massachusetts than the strip malls of Costa Mesa, California. What draws people to traditional small towns is difficult to define, so we usually call it "charm," and then bemoan the fact that they just don't build them the way they used to. Why they don't build them the way that way is something we seldom consider.

Tom Johnson 1986 Home Magazine

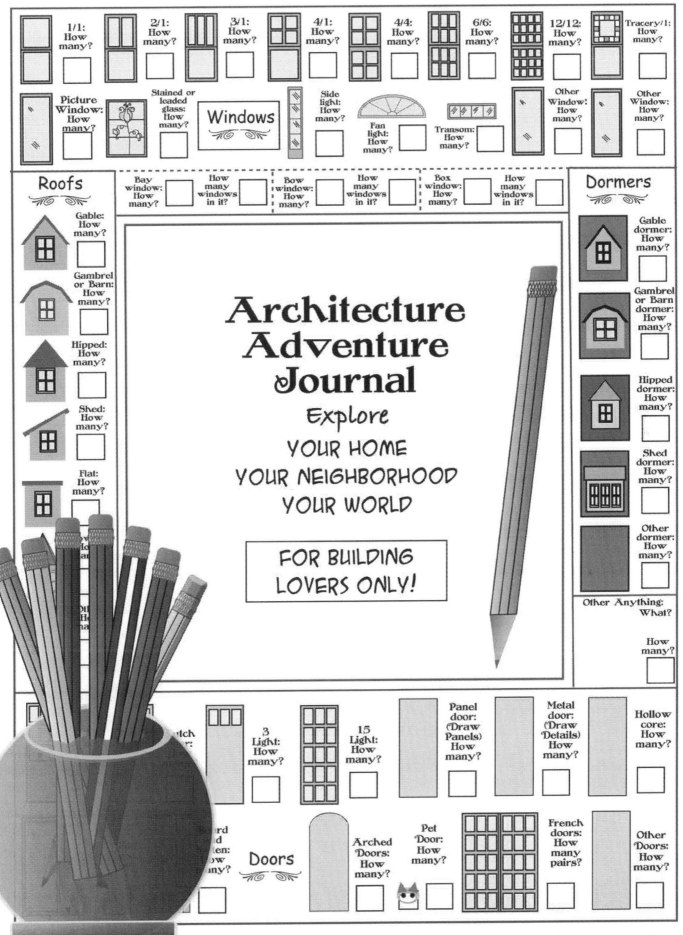

Windows

1/1: How many?

2/1: How many?

3/1: How many?

4/1: How many?

4/4: How many?

6/6: How many?

12/12: How many?

Tracery/1: How many?

Picture Window: How many?

Stained or leaded glass: How many?

Windows

Side light: How many?

Fan light: How many?

Transom: How many?

Other Window: How many?

Other Window: How many?

Bay window: How many?

How many windows in it?

Bow window: How many?

How many windows in it?

Box window: How many?

How many windows in it?

Roofs

Gable: How many?

Gambrel or Barn: How many?

Hipped: How many?

Shed: How many?

Flat: How many?

Dormers

Gable dormer: How many?

Gambrel or Barn dormer: How many?

Hipped dormer: How many?

Shed dormer: How many?

Other dormer: How many?

Other Anything: What?

How many?

Architecture Adventure Journal

Explore

YOUR HOME
YOUR NEIGHBORHOOD
YOUR WORLD

FOR BUILDING LOVERS ONLY!

Doors

3 Light: How many?

15 Light: How many?

Panel door: (Draw Panels) How many?

Metal door: (Draw Details) How many?

Hollow core: How many?

Arched Doors: How many?

Pet Door: How many?

French doors: How many pairs?

Other Doors: How many?

SHEILA COFFIN HARSHMAN

MAY YOUR
HOME BE
HAPPY.

Dear Friend,   19 August, 2012

The way we live is reflected in our homes and in the buildings around us. Many details of our everyday lives may disappear is we don't make note of them and when we want to tell our grandchildren what our lives were like they might be fascinated to look through this book.

You can explore more than just your own house with this book. I have included some extra pages so you can draw other buildings on your property, or other houses or buildings that interest you.

I've tried to keep the price low on these books as a special gift to those who simply love structures; I hope that you will buy a dozen copies, and that you draw every building that interests you! Be sure to date the pages and to put an address! And I hope that you will buy copies to give as gifts. I think people will be glad to have a record of their homes and of the places they love and that their children and grandchildren will enjoy the book they have sketched in.

Old and young love to make note of their homes and the other special places in their lives. I hope you, and those you give these books to, will enjoy them your whole lives.

HAVE FUN!

Love,
Sheila

A Good Building Directly Reflects the People Who Will Live In It... And No One Else

"SO LONG AS I BUILD FOR MYSELF, THE PATTERNS I USE WILL BE SIMPLE, AND HUMAN, AND FULL OF FEELING, BECAUSE I UNDERSTAND MY SITUATION.

BUT AS SOON AS A FEW PEOPLE BEGIN TO BUILD FOR 'THE MANY,' THEIR PATTERNS ABOUT WHAT IS NEEDED BECOME ABSTRACT; NO MATTER HOW WELL MEANING THEY ARE, THEIR IDEAS GRADUALLY GET OUT OF TOUCH WITH REALITY, BECAUSE THEY ARE NOT FACED DAILY WITH THE LIVING EXAMPLES OF WHAT THE PATTERNS SAY.

IF I BUILD A FIREPLACE FOR MYSELF, IT IS NATURAL FOR ME TO MAKE A PLACE TO PUT THE WOOD, A CORNER TO SIT IN, A MANTEL WIDE ENOUGH TO PUT THINGS ON, AN OPENING WHICH LETS THE FIRE DRAW.

BUT, IF I DESIGN FIREPLACES FOR OTHER PEOPLE -- NOT FOR MYSELF -- THEN I NEVER HAVE TO BUILD A FIRE IN THE FIREPLACES I DESIGN. GRADUALLY MY IDEAS BECOME MORE AND MORE INFLUENCED BY STYLE, AND SHAPE, AND CRAZY NOTIONS -- MY FEELING FOR THE SIMPLE BUSINESS OF MAKING FIRE LEAVES THE FIREPLACE ALTOGETHER."

PP. 235 - 236
A TIMELESS WAY OF BUILDING
CHRISTOPHER ALEXANDER
COPYRIGHT 1979

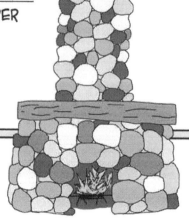

Table of Contents

Consider This...

"ENTRANCE ROOM

ARRIVING IN A BUILDING, OR LEAVING IT, YOU
NEED A ROOM TO PASS THROUGH, BOTH
INSIDE THE BUILDING AND OUTSIDE IT.
THIS IS THE ENTRANCE ROOM."
SOME ELEMENTS IN THIS TO CONSIDER ARE:
THE NEED FOR SHELTER OUTSIDE THE DOOR.
A SHELF OUTSIDE TO PUT PARCELS ON.
A SHELF JUST INSIDE AS A SORT OF LOADING
DOCK SO THINGS TO BE TAKEN OUT OF THE
HOUSE ARE NOT FORGOTTEN.
A PLACE FOR MUDDY BOOTS.
A PLACE FOR WET COATS.
A PATTERN LANGUAGE
CHRISTOPHER ALEXANDER @ 1977
P. 623

Table of Contents

Consider This...

DESIGNING A HOME IS NOT ABOUT AN
ARROGANT STRANGER WITH A HEAD
FULL OF THEIR OWN STRANGE IDEAS
WHO CHARGES YOU A SUBSTANTIAL
SUM FOR DRAWING PICTURES OF WHAT
HE WANTS FOR YOU.
A HOME BECOMES A HOME WHEN THE
OWNER STANDS ON THEIR PROPERTY
AND BEGINS TO IMAGINE AND DREAM
ABOUT WHO THEY ARE AND THEIR
OWN UNIQUE SITUATION.

YOU

Today's Date:_____

Name: _____

Date of Birth: _____ Age: _____

Where You Were Born: _____

Address where your family lived when you

were born:_____

Street Address Now: _____

City/Town: _____

Zip Code: _____

State: _____

County (Not Country): _____

Country: _____

FATHER

Your father's name: _____

Date of Birth: _____

Place of Birth; _____

His father's name/

Your Grandfather: _____

Date of Birth: _____

Place of Birth; _____

His mother's name/

Your Grandmother: _____

Date of Birth: _____

Place of Birth; _____

His Brothers and Sisters/Your Aunts and Uncles:

_____

_____

_____

MOTHER

Your mother's name: _____

Date of Birth: _____

Place of Birth; _____

Her father's name/

Your Grandfather: _____

Date of Birth: _____

Place of Birth; _____

Her mother's name/

Your Grandmother: _____

Date of Birth: _____

Place of Birth; _____

Her Brothers and Sisters/Your Aunts and Uncles:

_____

_____

_____

13

WHO LIVES WITH YOU?

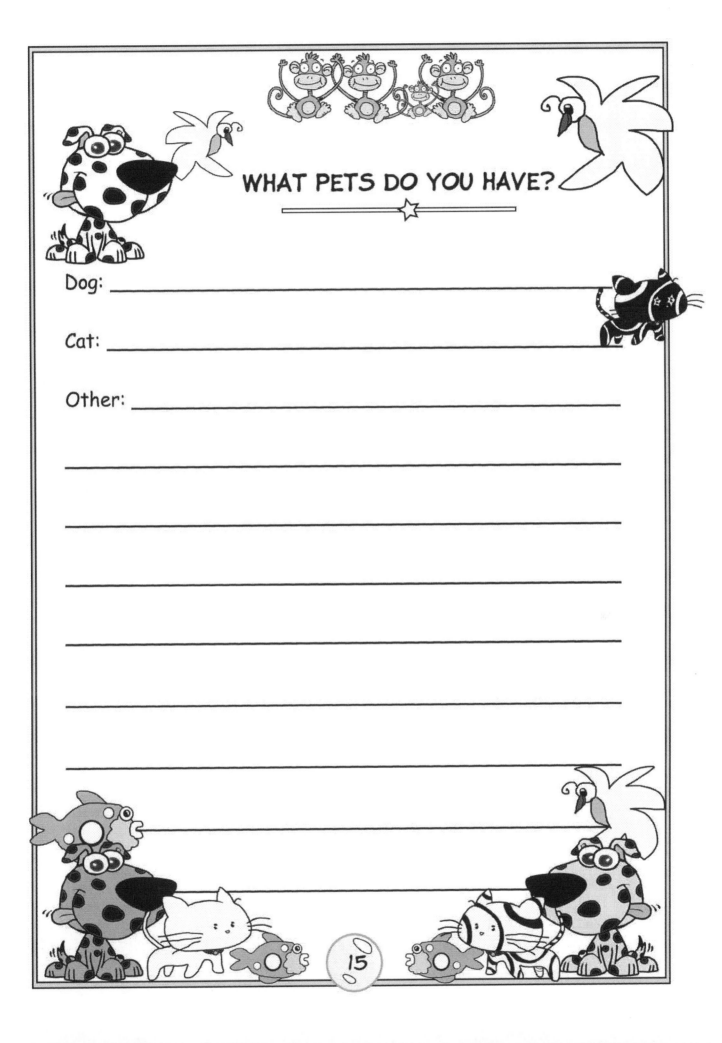

WHAT PETS DO YOU HAVE?

Dog: _____

Cat: _____

Other: _____

_____

_____

_____

_____

_____

_____

_____

A LITTLE MORE ABOUT
WHERE YOU LIVE

Population of your city or town: _____

Latitude of your city or town: _____

Longitude of your city or town: _____

What is near your home? - {Within ten (10) miles.}

Mountains		Stream	
Hills		City	
Flat		Suburb	
Sometimes snowy		Country	
Tropical		Walk to school	
Desert		Walk to stores	
Prairie		Walk to Church	
Ocean		Parents walk to work	
Lake		A lot of wood fences	
River		A lot of stone walls	

HOW FAR?

How far away is a grocery store?_____

How far away is a library? _____

How far away is a school? _____

How far away is a police department? _____

How far away is a fire department? _____

How far away is a church? _____

How far away is a hardware store? _____

Where do you go? And how far away is it?

1. _____

2. _____

3. _____

4. _____

5. _____

WALKING

WHAT ARE SOME THINGS YOU CAN
WALK TO FROM YOUR HOME?

THE Did You Know? SECTION

SOME THINGS YOU'LL WANT TO KNOW:

☆ <u>Elevation</u> means the front, back, or side of something.

☆ <u>Floor Plan</u> is a drawing showing the inside of a building as if you were looking at it from above.

☆ <u>Plot Plan</u> is a drawing that shows the layout of the land a property sits on as if you were looking from above.

An apostrophe ' means "feet"

A quotation mark " means "inches"

If one of the dimensions of a room are 12 feet 4 inches it would be written like this:

12'- 4"

OLD HOUSES

An Interesting thing about old houses

Old houses were built to change. When families grew houses grew. When families needs changed - their houses changed. Older houses were built so that they automatically provided for changing situations. They were built with steep roofs. There was space up in the rafters for people to live and to store things.

When people other than the owner interject their opinions or regulations into the building process the result is ruined homes, towns, cities, and families.

Our poverty or our wealth as a nation is reflected in our homes: New houses often have shallow roof pitches and no rafters - they often have trusses instead. Trusses limit how a family can use their space. People have to store their property away from their homes and to spend money for storage.

A STEEP ROOF PROVIDES
ANOTHER ENTIRE FLOOR
FOR LIVING AND STORAGE.

A SHALLOW ROOF IS
WASTEFUL AND PROVIDES
FEWER OPPORTUNITIES.

TRUSSES GO AWAY!

IT DOESN'T FEEL LIKE A SMALL PRICE TO ME!

THE ONLY REAL DISADVANTAGE OF ROOF TRUSSES IS THAT THE HOMEOWNER ENDS UP WITH LESS USABLE SPACE IN THE ATTIC AREA; A VERY SMALL PRICE TO PAY!

Benefits of Roof Trusses

by I.M.A. Lazy Carpenter

"Conventional roof rafters and ceiling joists are less often used in new home construction these days. In fact, nearly 80% of homes built today use pre-manufactured roof trusses instead of traditional rafters to support the roof!

Roof trusses are pre-fabricated, triangulated wood structures which are built in a factory and carefully designed to carry the load of a home's roof to the outside walls. They are then shipped to the construction site and installed using a crane after the home's walls have been framed.

Ask most builders today and they will tell you that engineered roof trusses are the only way to go and are far better than the old roof frames. The primary benefits of using pre-fabricated roof trusses are cost savings and construction speed.

The flexibility in the roof design and complexity that roof trusses enable have also made them increasingly popular. With today's home styles, more complex roof designs, angles, cross gables and other features have added cost, which can be at least partially offset by using pre-manufactured roof trusses rather than building a roof frame on site.

The only real disadvantage of roof trusses is that the homeowner ends up with less usable space in the attic area; a very small price to pay!"

Consider This...
How Much Have We
Forgotten?

"AT ONE TIME IT WOULD HAVE BEEN UNTHINKABLE TO BUILD ANY ROOM, EXCEPT A STABLE OR A WORKSHED, WITHOUT WINDOWS ON TWO SIDES.

IN OUR OWN TIME, ALL KNOWLEDGE OF THIS PATTERN IS FORGOTTEN."

"THERE IS NOT A SINGLE BUILDING BUILT IN RECENT TIMES, NOR A SINGLE PART OF A CITY LAID OUT BY PLANNERS*, IN WHICH SUCH TRIVIAL MISTAKES -- CAUSED BY THE LOSS OF PATTERNS - CANNOT BE DESCRIBED A HUNDREDFOLD."

<u>A TIMELESS WAY OF BUILDING</u>
CHRISTOPHER ALEXANDER @ 1979 P. 235

*To entrust the building of a town or city to a bunch of **thugs who do not <u>OWN</u> the land they are regulating is to invite disaster. Great communities, towns, and cities were built one building at a time by people of independence and genius. "Planning and Zoning" are ideas right from the <u>Communist Manifesto</u> by Karl Marx and are of the tools used to enslave people.

**Thugs:

"It's said that 'power corrupts,' but actually it's more true that power attracts the corruptible. The sane are usually attracted by other things than power.

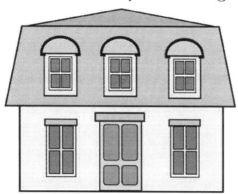

The tyrant, though, seeks mastery, for which he is insatiable, implacable."
The Postman
David Brin @1997

Foundations

The foundation is the base upon which the whole building rests. It is usually made of stone or cement and rests in part, or wholly below the surface of the ground.

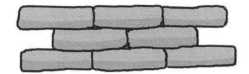

Bricks: might be red or yellow.

Stone

Cement/concrete blocks - may have stucco on them.

Wood post or pier

Metal post

Cement Slab

Consider This...

"CAR CONNECTION

THE PROCESS OF ARRIVING IN A
HOUSE, AND LEAVING IT, IS
FUNDAMENTAL TO OUR DAILY LIVES;
AND VERY OFTEN IT INVOLVES A CAR.
BUT THE PLACE WHERE CARS
CONNECT TO HOUSES, FAR FROM
BEING IMPORTANT AND BEAUTIFUL, IS
OFTEN TO ONE SIDE AND
NEGLECTED."
<u>A PATTERN LANGUAGE</u>
CHRISTOPHER ALEXANDER @ 1977
P. 554

Stairs

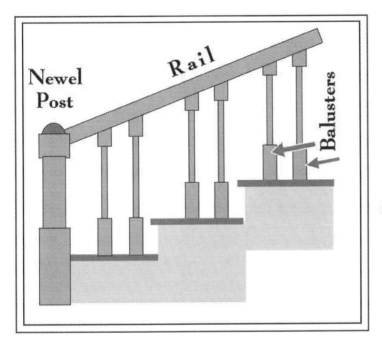

Newel Post

Rail

Balusters

7/11 is the big stair formula to remember.

This means that the height or "rise" of the stair is seven inches and the depth or "run" (the place you put your foot) of the stair is eleven inches.

NOTE: Making the rise a fraction of an inch less than seven inches is actually better than a true seven inch step. If you make your stairs taller than seven inches you may regret it for a very long time.

This is how stairs are figured: Measure the entire height of your space from the first floor to the EVENTUAL height of the finished floor above it. Divide this height by seven (inches - a good stair height.). If the math does not come out evenly make each stair EXACTLY the same height while keeping the height as close to seven inches, or less, (never more) as possible.

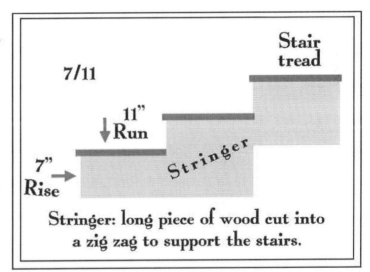

7/11

Stair tread

11"
Run

7"
Rise

Stringer

Stringer: long piece of wood cut into a zig zag to support the stairs.

Consider This...

"OPEN STAIRS

THE PATTERN OF MANY OPEN
STAIRS, LEADING OFF THE PUBLIC
STREETS, DIRECT TO PRIVATE DOORS,
HAS IN ITS NATURE THE FACT OF
INDEPENDENCE, FREE COMINGS AND
GOINGS."
A PATTERN LANGUAGE
CHRISTOPHER ALEXANDER @ 1977
P. 742

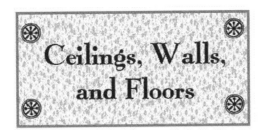

Ceilings, Walls, and Floors

As you work on your floor plans you might want to note what your Ceilings, Walls, and Floors are made of. Some Possibilities are:

- Ceilings: Plaster, Wood, Sheet Rock

- Walls: Plaster, Wood, Sheet Rock, Brick, Stone

- Floors: Wood, Ceramic Tile, Vinyl

Consider This...

"WARM COLORS

NATURAL WOOD, SUNLIGHT, BRIGHT COLORS ARE WARM. IN SOME WAY, THE WARMTH OF THE COLORS IN A ROOM MAKES A GREAT DEAL OF DIFFERENCE BETWEEN COMFORT AND DISCOMFORT."
<u>A PATTERN LANGUAGE</u>
CHRISTOPHER ALEXANDER @ 1977
P. 1153

SO...
WHEN SHOPPING FOR PAINT...
YOU MIGHT JUST SAY NO TO
AVOCADO
AND TOMATO!

Warmth &
Sunlight

30

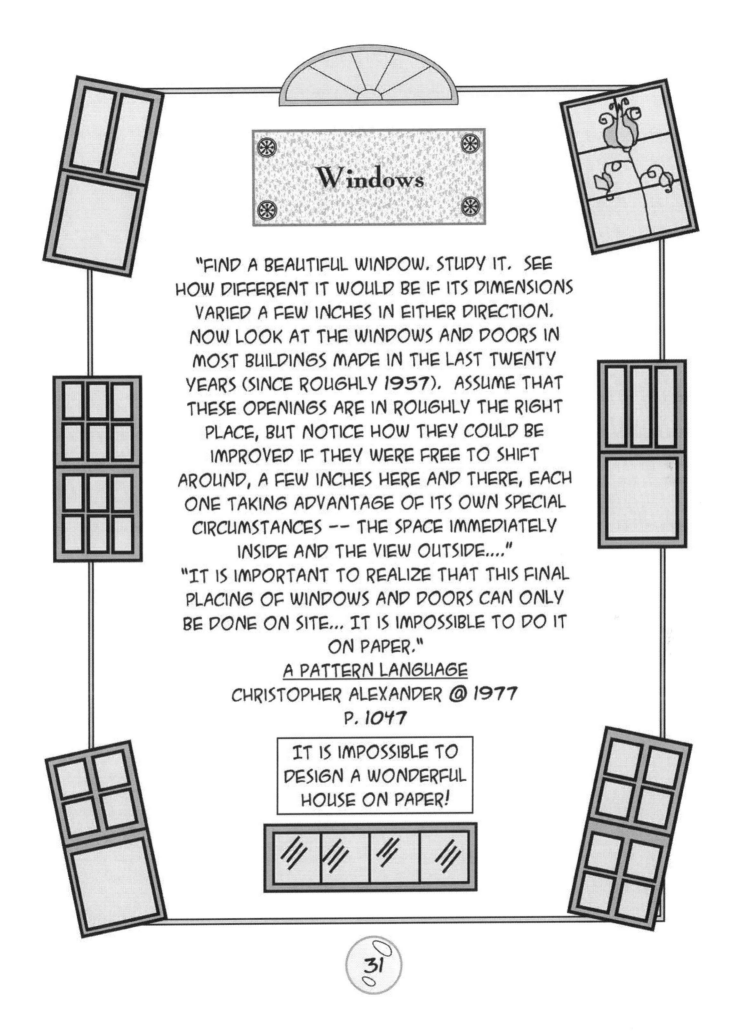

Windows

"FIND A BEAUTIFUL WINDOW. STUDY IT. SEE HOW DIFFERENT IT WOULD BE IF ITS DIMENSIONS VARIED A FEW INCHES IN EITHER DIRECTION. NOW LOOK AT THE WINDOWS AND DOORS IN MOST BUILDINGS MADE IN THE LAST TWENTY YEARS (SINCE ROUGHLY 1957). ASSUME THAT THESE OPENINGS ARE IN ROUGHLY THE RIGHT PLACE, BUT NOTICE HOW THEY COULD BE IMPROVED IF THEY WERE FREE TO SHIFT AROUND, A FEW INCHES HERE AND THERE, EACH ONE TAKING ADVANTAGE OF ITS OWN SPECIAL CIRCUMSTANCES -- THE SPACE IMMEDIATELY INSIDE AND THE VIEW OUTSIDE...."

"IT IS IMPORTANT TO REALIZE THAT THIS FINAL PLACING OF WINDOWS AND DOORS CAN ONLY BE DONE ON SITE... IT IS IMPOSSIBLE TO DO IT ON PAPER."

A PATTERN LANGUAGE
CHRISTOPHER ALEXANDER @ 1977
P. 1047

IT IS IMPOSSIBLE TO DESIGN A WONDERFUL HOUSE ON PAPER!

31

WINDOW ANATOMY

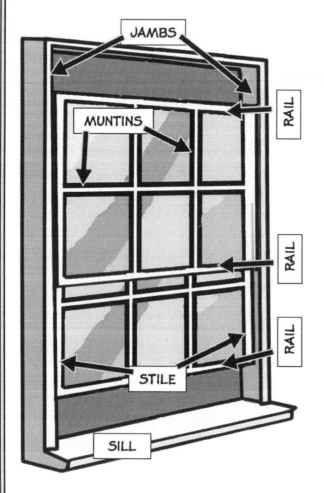

- **Rail:**
  Rails are the horizontal members of the sash. Every sash has a top and a bottom rail. Rails located at the center of a double-hung window opening are known as meeting rails.
- **Jamb:**
  Jambs are the main vertical members that form the sides of a window.
- **Stile:**
  Stiles are the main vertical members in the framework of a sash, found at the sides of a window.
- **Glazing (Or Lights):**
  Glazing is a term used for the process of mounting glass into windows and doors and also refers to the glass or plastic panes themselves.
- **Muntin:**
  Muntins are individual pieces of wood that help hold window panes in the sash and divide a window opening into smaller sections.

Sash:
The frame of the window that actually holds the glass in place.

GLASS PANES MIGHT ALSO BE CALLED "GLAZING," OR "LIGHTS."

WINDOWS –
SOME EXAMPLES

Casement:
May have a crank. Sometimes used in modern construction. They may flank plate glass/picture windows.

Jalousie:
Like shutters made of glass.

Sliding:

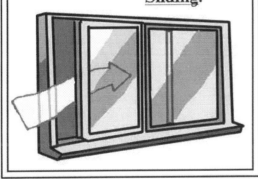

Transom:
This may have true divided lights and be very beautiful. Some transoms do not open.

Awning:
May have a crank. Often used in modern construction in basements.

STAINED GLASS

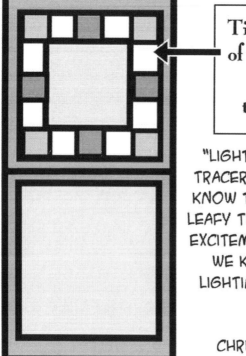

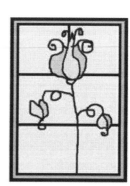

Tiny panes of glass are called tracery.

"LIGHT FILTERED THROUGH LEAVES, OR TRACERY, IS WONDERFUL. BUT WHY? WE KNOW THAT LIGHT FILTERING THROUGH A LEAFY TREE IS VERY PLEASANT -- IT LENDS EXCITEMENT, CHEERFULNESS, GAIETY; AND WE KNOW THAT AREAS OF UNIFORM LIGHTING CREATE DULL, UNINTERESTING SPACES."
A PATTERN LANGUAGE
CHRISTOPHER ALEXANDER @ 1977
P. 1106

"WE HAVE A NATURAL DESIRE TO DIFFUSE LIGHT WITH LAMPSHADES OR INDIRECT LIGHTING, SO THAT THE IMAGES CREATED BY THE LIGHT WILL BE 'SOFTER'..."
A PATTERN LANGUAGE
CHRISTOPHER ALEXANDER @ 1977
P. 1106

The Joyless Revolution:
Depressed? Don't be duped. Throw out your fluorescent bulbs! Fluorescent lights are about the worst things yet. They are damaging to your eyes, your nervous system, and they pollute! Choose natural windows, incandescent lighting, and candles. Choose joy!

The Classic

Double-hung Window

A double hung window is probably the most versatile of all windows.
This window has two movable sashes that slide up and down.

IN THIS WINDOW THE GLASS PANES ARE HELD IN PLACE BY WOOD ON THE INSIDE.
ON THE OUTSIDE TINY BITS OF METAL CALLED "POINTS" ARE USED ALONG WITH A GLAZING PUTTY.
THE PUTTY FORMS A SLIGHTLY FLEXIBLE SEAL THAT IS ABLE TO TOLERATE EXTREMES OF TEMPERATURE.

Window glazing tool.

This is a 6/6 window - called a six over six, double hung, true divided light window.

If one of these panes of glass is broken it is easy to replace it with glass, putty, and simple household tools.

Consider This...

"WINDOW PLACE

EVERYBODY LOVES WINDOW SEATS, BAY WINDOWS, AND BIG WINDOWS WITH LOW SILLS AND COMFORTABLE CHAIRS DRAWN UP TO THEM. IT IS EASY TO THINK OF THESE KINDS OF PLACES AS LUXURIES, AND WHICH WE ARE NO LONGER LUCKY ENOUGH TO BE ABLE TO AFFORD. IN FACT THE MATTER IS MORE URGENT. THESE KINDS OF WINDOWS WHICH CREATE 'PLACES' NEXT TO THEM ARE NOT SIMPLY LUXURIES; THEY ARE NECESSARY. A ROOM WHICH DOES NOT HAVE A PLACE LIKE THIS SELDOM ALLOWS YOU TO FEEL COMFORTABLE OR PERFECTLY AT EASE. INDEED, A ROOM WITHOUT A WINDOW PLACE MAY KEEP YOU IN A STATE OF PERPETUAL UNRESOLVED CONFLICT AND TENSION – SLIGHT, PERHAPS, BUT DEFINITE."
A PATTERN LANGUAGE
CHRISTOPHER ALEXANDER @ 1977
P. 833

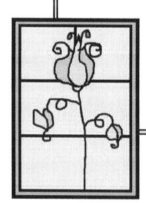

"ONE OF A WINDOW'S MOST IMPORTANT FUNCTIONS IS TO PUT YOU IN TOUCH WITH THE OUTDOORS. IF THE SILL IS TOO HIGH IT CUTS YOU OFF."
A PATTERN LANGUAGE
CHRISTOPHER ALEXANDER @ 1977
P. 1051

"THE 'RIGHT' HEIGHT FOR A WINDOW SILL IS ASTONISHINGLY LOW. OUR EXPERIENCES SHOW THAT SILLS WHICH ARE 13 OR 14 INCHES FROM THE FLOOR ARE PERFECT.... MOST WINDOWS HAVE SILL HEIGHTS OF 30 INCHES, OR SO, SO THAT WHEN YOU SIT DOWN BY THEM YOU CANNOT SEE THE GROUND RIGHT NEAR THE WINDOW. THIS IS UNUSUALLY FRUSTRATING -- YOU ALMOST HAVE TO STAND UP TO GET A COMPLETE VIEW."
A PATTERN LANGUAGE
CHRISTOPHER ALEXANDER @ 1977
P. 1051

FAKE DIVIDER CALLED A "GRILL" THAT FITS OVER PLATE GLASS.

THINGS YOU CAN EXPECT IN A MODERN DOUBLE-HUNG WINDOW INCLUDE:

1. PLASTIC
2. METAL
3. NOT MADE WITH SMALL PIECES OF GLASS BUT LARGE PLATE GLASS.
4. FITTED WITH FAKE "GRILLS" OVER THE PLATE GLASS IN EACH SASH.
5. MADE WITH DOUBLE, OR TRIPLE PIECES OF GLASS WITH ALL SORTS OF GASKETS TO SEAL THEM AND GAS IN BETWEEN THE SHEETS OF GLASS.
6. THIS WINDOW CANNOT BE REPAIRED WHEN IT FAILS. THE ENTIRE WINDOW WILL NEED TO BE REPLACED BY A GOOD CARPENTER.

In building, as in so many things...
If something is worth imitating - it is worth having the genuine article! An authentic item may bring so much pleasure that it is worth obtaining only the real, the original, and not the phony. And it may be something to resent, this insistence on filling our buildings with sub-standard, disposable building elements that never give us any joy but rob us of simple happiness in our everyday lives.

"WHEN PLATE GLASS WINDOWS BECAME POSSIBLE, PEOPLE THOUGHT THAT THEY WOULD PUT US MORE DIRECTLY IN TOUCH WITH NATURE. IN FACT, THEY DO THE OPPOSITE. THEY ALIENATE US FROM THE VIEW. THE SMALLER THE WINDOWS ARE, THE SMALLER THE PANES ARE, THE MORE INTENSELY WINDOWS HELP CONNECT US WITH WHAT IS ON THE OTHER SIDE."
A PATTERN LANGUAGE
CHRISTOPHER ALEXANDER @ 1977
P. 1109

Consider This...

"INTERIOR WINDOWS

...THERE ARE MANY CASES WHEN AN
INDOOR SPACE NEEDS A
CONNECTING WINDOW TO AN
INDOOR SPACE."
A PATTERN LANGUAGE
CHRISTOPHER ALEXANDER @ 1977
P. 898

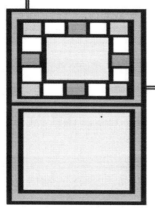

40

The Replacement
Window Scam

You've been fooled. The Replacement Window epidemic is just a conspiracy to take your money.
Ken Roginski: www.oldhouseguy.com

Windows are the eyes of a house. They are the most important character defining feature creating the greatest visual impact on the overall appearance of a house.

Because of this, the decision to replace an original wood window must be carefully considered and understood. We all want to reduce our heating bills and save money. How can we do that with 100 year old, drafty windows that are in bad shape? You can – there is no need to compromise. Read on and see.

The public has been brain-washed by marketers. Even an eight year old "knows" you need to replace your old windows to save energy and lower your heating bill. What else can you expect with all the advertisements and promotions manipulating the public? This is big business and high sales commissions are paid to highly trained people to convince you to replace your windows. Their livelihoods depend on these sales.

The Replacement Window Scam

Additionally, with the rush to conserve energy and make everything "green," misinformation from the current sustainability movement has imbedded in our minds the idea that all old windows are NOT efficient and NOT green. Financial incentives such as tax credits for home efficiency improvements have escalated the situation to a frightening degree, making old windows the most vulnerable element of a building. The result – the consumer spends money that will never be regained – a very bad investment. Additionally, the character of the house is destroyed forever.

A common and often exaggerated reason for replacement windows is that new windows will significantly reduce heating costs. This is wrong! **Studies have indicated that in most cases, approximately 10% of the heating loss of a building is through windows. The remaining 90% loss is through gaps** in roofs, walls, floors, and chimneys, with roofs being the greatest culprit. These other areas of heat loss can be resolved at a much lower cost and result in much more savings on your heating bill than replacing windows.

Following this model, **reducing the heat loss through windows by 50% will only result in a 5% decrease in the overall heat loss** in the building and your heating bill. Again - pay close attention to advertisements stating, a 50% reduction in your heating bill.

The Replacement
Window Scam

It is all a tactic to get you excited and interested to save heating expenses. It is NOT a 50% savings of your heating bill – IT IS a 50% savings of the 10% heat loss through all of your windows, which will save you 5% off your heating bill. Even with this in mind, keeping the heat in and the cold out are still prime wintertime goals. However, both goals can be met with your existing original windows. Keeping the heat in, means insulation measured in R-value (measurement of a materials resistance to heat flow).

An old window coupled with a storm window will give you a higher R-value than a double-glazed replacement. This is because there is more air space between the storm window and the inside window than between the two tightly squeezed panes (double pane) of glass in a replacement thermo pane window. Believe it or not, air is one of the best insulators. Since molecules are so far apart in air, heat cannot be transferred. Therefore, the **three inches of air space you have between the two pieces of glass performs as a very good insulator.**

The Replacement
Window Scam

The Science of Drafts and Where They Come From

What about drafts? **You can feel the same draft with brand new "top of the line" windows** as well as with your old windows. The reason for this is *Convection.* This is how it works. Glass is a great conductor. The warm air in your house contacts cold window glass where it cools and then draws more warm air to it. This continues on and on until convection currents are created throughout the room and, perhaps throughout the entire house.

This draft feeling is created only because the product GLASS is used in a window. If you really want to prevent drafts, you can use wood instead, however you will not be able to see outside.

Use of interior shutters, shades, or curtains can solve the draft problem by blocking off the glass from the warmed room air. An additional layer of glass (storm window) which creates an air space between the two glasses will help; however, you are still using glass, and heat will still be drawn to it, although not as much.

Ken Roginski

www.oldhouseguy.com

"IF YOU REALLY WANT TO PREVENT DRAFTS, YOU CAN USE WOOD INSTEAD, (OF GLASS) HOWEVER YOU WILL NOT BE ABLE TO SEE OUTSIDE."

After one hundred years, the old classic, double hung, wooden window made up of tiny panes of glass still has half of its life ahead of it.

REPLACEMENT WINDOWS ARE NOT GREEN...

AND WILL NOT SIGNIFICANTLY LOWER YOUR HEATING BILLS. YOU HAVE BEEN TRICKED INTO BELIEVING THIS BY SCOUNDRELS PAID WITH YOUR OWN TAX DOLLARS.

Versus one hundred years of replacement windows cluttering up the dump.

And this is just replacing one window!

Consider This...

"SOLID DOORS WITH GLASS

AS OFTEN AS POSSIBLE BUILD DOORS
WITH GLAZING IN THEM, SO THAT
THE UPPER HALF, AT LEAST, ALLOWS
YOU TO SEE THROUGH THEM."
<u>A PATTERN LANGUAGE</u>
CHRISTOPHER ALEXANDER @ 1977
P. 1103

46

DOORS

INTERIOR DOORS WITH WINDOWS:

"A GLAZED DOOR (ONE WITH WINDOWS IN IT) ALLOWS
FOR A MORE GRACEFUL ENTRANCE INTO A ROOM AND
FOR A MORE GRACEFUL RECEPTION BY PEOPLE IN THE
ROOM, BECAUSE IT ALLOWS BOTH PARTIES TO
GET READY FOR EACH OTHER.
IT ALSO ALLOWS FOR DIFFERENT DEGREES OF PRIVACY....
AND MOST IMPORTANT, IT GIVES THE FEELING THAT
EVERYONE IN THE BUILDING IS CONNECTED --
NOT ISOLATED IN PRIVATE ROOMS."
A PATTERN LANGUAGE
CHRISTOPHER ALEXANDER @ 1977
P. 1103

DOOR ANATOMY

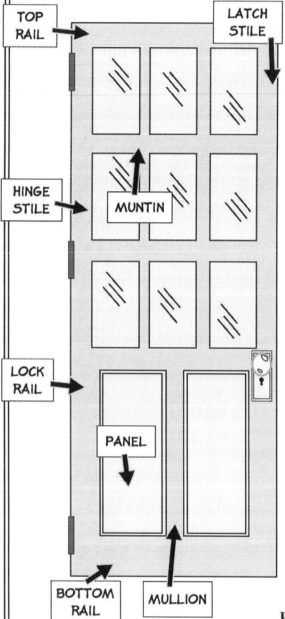

TOP RAIL

LATCH STILE

HINGE STILE

MUNTIN

LOCK RAIL

PANEL

BOTTOM RAIL

MULLION

- **Rail:**
  Horizontal members of the door. Every door has a top, latch, and bottom rail.
- **Stile:**
  Stiles are the main vertical members in the framework of a sash, found at the sides of a window.
- **Glazing (Or Panes, Or Lights):**
  Glazing is a term used for the process of mounting glass into windows and doors and also refers to the glass or panes themselves.
- **Panel:**
  Flat or molded piece of wood that is inset in grooves in rails, stiles and mullions in a multi-panel door.
- **Mullion:**
  Pieces of wood that separate panels in a multi-panel door.
- **Muntin:**
  Individual pieces of wood that help hold window panes in the sash and divide a window opening into smaller sections.

Helpful Tip:
Try to arrange your home so that all of your doors are thirty-six inches wide (36") You might be surprised at what a difference it makes! I have used 36" French doors between rooms and been very happy. Entering through the center of a door, rather than walking around an edge is a very nice experience.

GLASS DOOR
ANATOMY

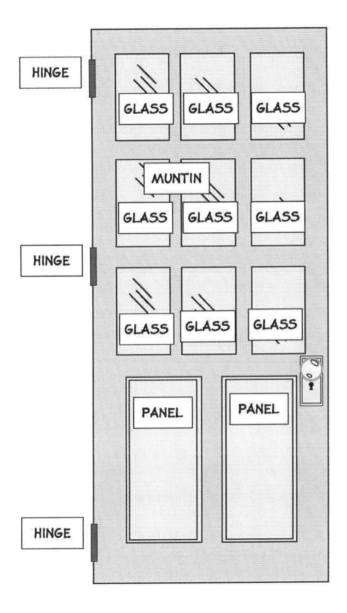

This is a nine light door - meaning that it has nine panes of glass in it.
A door with glass in it is called a glazed door.

This is a standard door with true divided lights. It has nine small panes of glass separated by wooden muntins. Doors, as in windows have the glass panes (or glaze or lights) held in place by wood on the inside. On the outside tiny bits of metal called "points" are used along with a glazing putty. The putty forms a slightly flexible seal that is able to tolerate extremes of temperature.

WHEN WINDOWS AND DOORS MEET

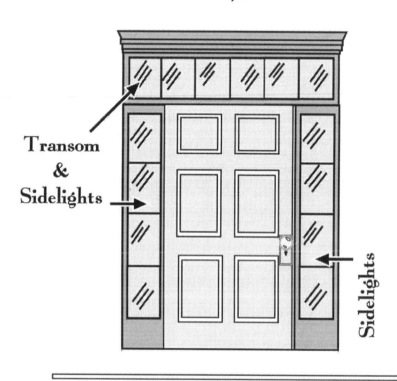

Transom & Sidelights

Sidelights

Fan light & Sidelights

Sidelights

SOME DOOR EXAMPLES

Dutch door

The top and bottom of this door open independently.

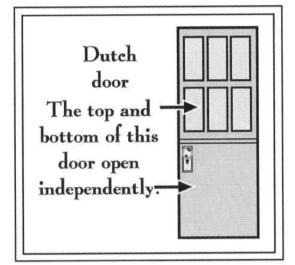

Fifteen light door.

This door has fifteen small panes of glass.

Pet door

French doors

These doors open away from each other at the center.

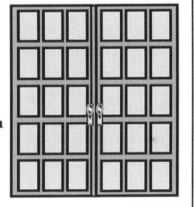

Board and Batten door

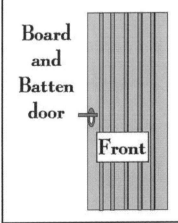

Front

Small wood strips called battens are placed to cover the space between the boards that comprise the door.

Back

The boards are often held together with a "Z" brace in back.

"ATTIC TO ME, MEANS
'A ROOM IN THE ROOF.'"
MARY HARSHMAN, AGE ELEVEN.
MARY LIVES IN AN OLD
VICTORIAN HOUSE.

52

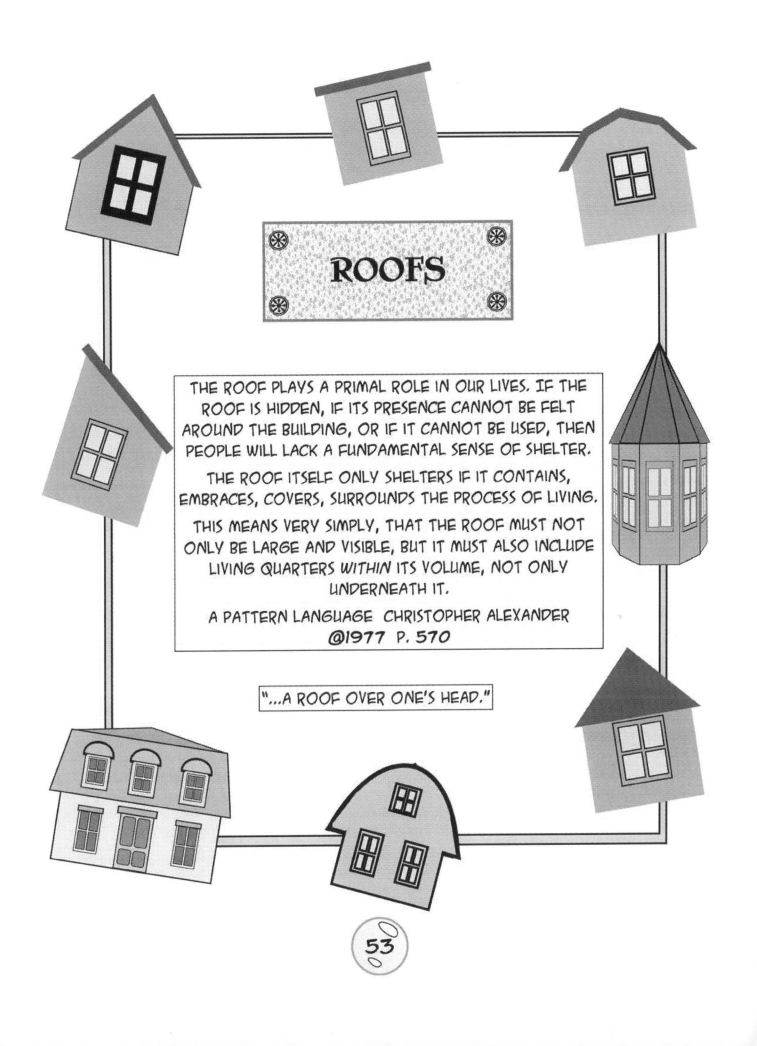

ROOFS

THE ROOF PLAYS A PRIMAL ROLE IN OUR LIVES. IF THE ROOF IS HIDDEN, IF ITS PRESENCE CANNOT BE FELT AROUND THE BUILDING, OR IF IT CANNOT BE USED, THEN PEOPLE WILL LACK A FUNDAMENTAL SENSE OF SHELTER.

THE ROOF ITSELF ONLY SHELTERS IF IT CONTAINS, EMBRACES, COVERS, SURROUNDS THE PROCESS OF LIVING.

THIS MEANS VERY SIMPLY, THAT THE ROOF MUST NOT ONLY BE LARGE AND VISIBLE, BUT IT MUST ALSO INCLUDE LIVING QUARTERS *WITHIN* ITS VOLUME, NOT ONLY UNDERNEATH IT.

A PATTERN LANGUAGE CHRISTOPHER ALEXANDER @1977 P. 570

"...A ROOF OVER ONE'S HEAD."

Hipped Roof

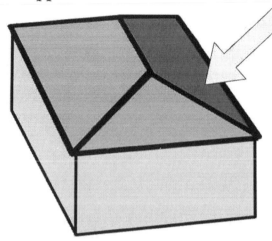

When you look at a hipped roof you will notice that it looks like a standard gable roof that has had its ends sheared off.

Many people like the look of this roof. A drawback to it is that the attic space is largely lost due to the fact that there are no vertical faces to this roof and with no vertical faces, such as those a standard gable roof has, there are no places to put windows (unless dormers are added) so whatever attic space the house has is a space with no windows.

Mansard Roof

This entire upper part of the roof remains largely unseen. This upper roof is like a tiny, fairly flat hipped roof.

A Mansard roof has windows in its almost-vertical sides. This roof frames the attic giving it the most useful and light-filled space of any roof. Many existing examples of the mansard roof are finished with thin layers of a type of stone called "slate." Look carefully when you see a mansard roof to see if it is slate. Slate is a very durable roof covering.

ROOFS

	Gable Roof	Gable, _____, _____, _____
	Gambrel or "Barn" Roof	Gambrel, _____, _____, _____
	Hipped Roof	Hipped, _____, _____, _____
	Shed Roof	Shed, _____, _____, _____
	Flat Roof	Flat, _____, _____, _____
	Mansard Roof	Mansard, _____, _____, _____
	Bow Roof	Bow, _____, _____, _____
	Tower	Tower, _____, _____, _____

ROOFS

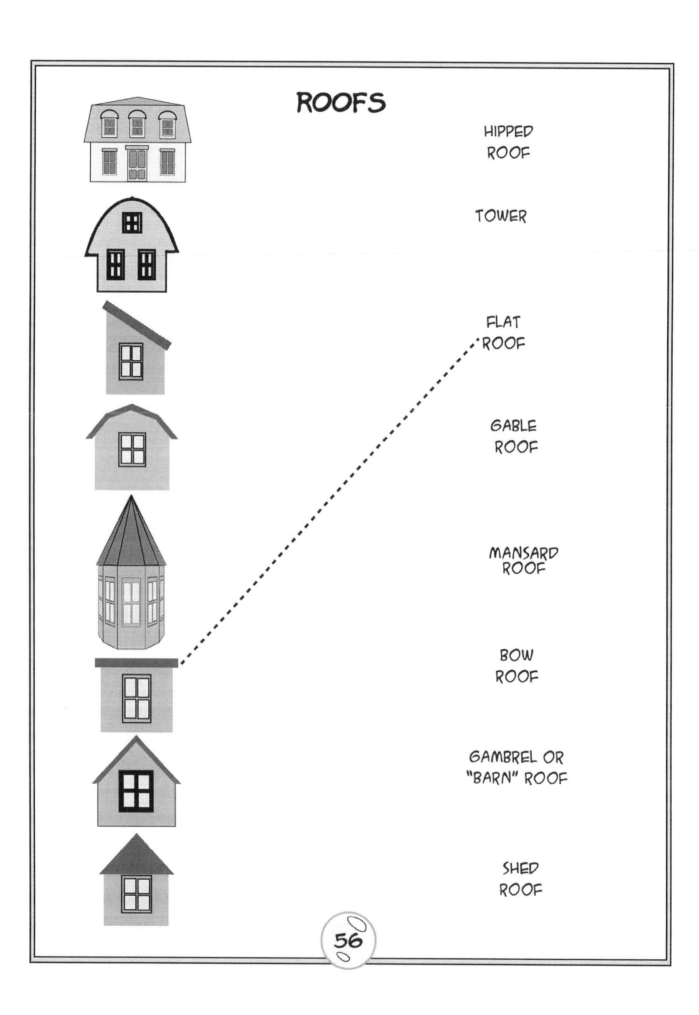

HIPPED
ROOF

TOWER

FLAT
ROOF

GABLE
ROOF

MANSARD
ROOF

BOW
ROOF

GAMBREL OR
"BARN" ROOF

SHED
ROOF

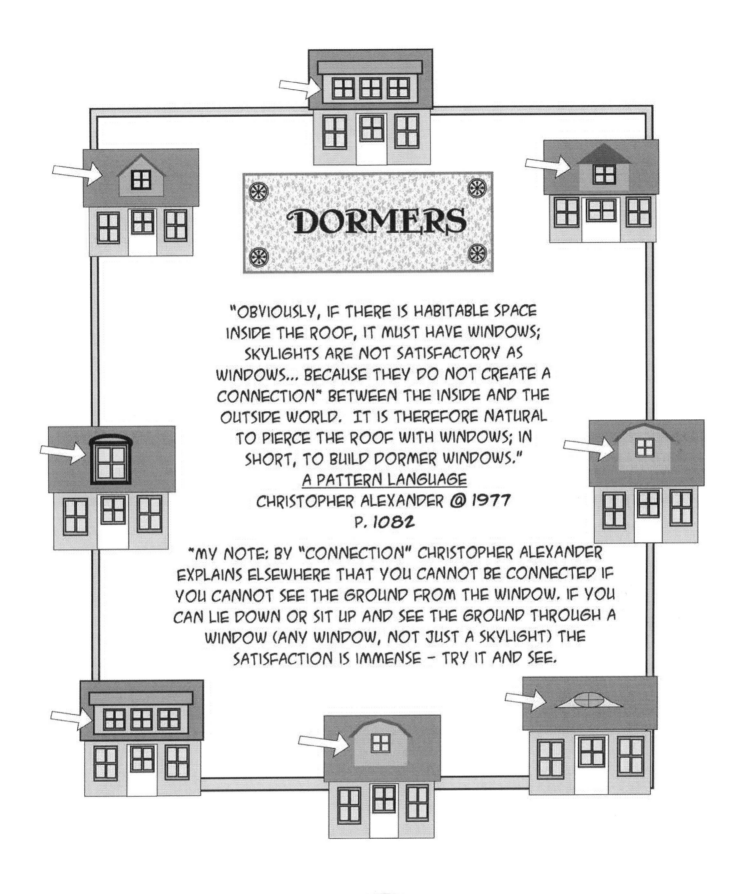

DORMERS

"OBVIOUSLY, IF THERE IS HABITABLE SPACE INSIDE THE ROOF, IT MUST HAVE WINDOWS; SKYLIGHTS ARE NOT SATISFACTORY AS WINDOWS... BECAUSE THEY DO NOT CREATE A CONNECTION* BETWEEN THE INSIDE AND THE OUTSIDE WORLD. IT IS THEREFORE NATURAL TO PIERCE THE ROOF WITH WINDOWS; IN SHORT, TO BUILD DORMER WINDOWS."
A PATTERN LANGUAGE
CHRISTOPHER ALEXANDER @ 1977
P. 1082

*MY NOTE: BY "CONNECTION" CHRISTOPHER ALEXANDER EXPLAINS ELSEWHERE THAT YOU CANNOT BE CONNECTED IF YOU CANNOT SEE THE GROUND FROM THE WINDOW. IF YOU CAN LIE DOWN OR SIT UP AND SEE THE GROUND THROUGH A WINDOW (ANY WINDOW, NOT JUST A SKYLIGHT) THE SATISFACTION IS IMMENSE – TRY IT AND SEE.

DORMERS

GABLE DORMER

Gable, _____

_____

_____

GAMBREL OR "BARN" DORMER

Gambrel/
Barn, _____

_____

_____

HIPPED DORMER

Hipped, _____

_____

_____

ARCH-TOPPED DORMER

Arch-topped _____

_____

_____

SHED DORMER

Shed, _____

_____

_____

EYEBROW DORMER

Eyebrow, _____

_____

_____

DORMERS

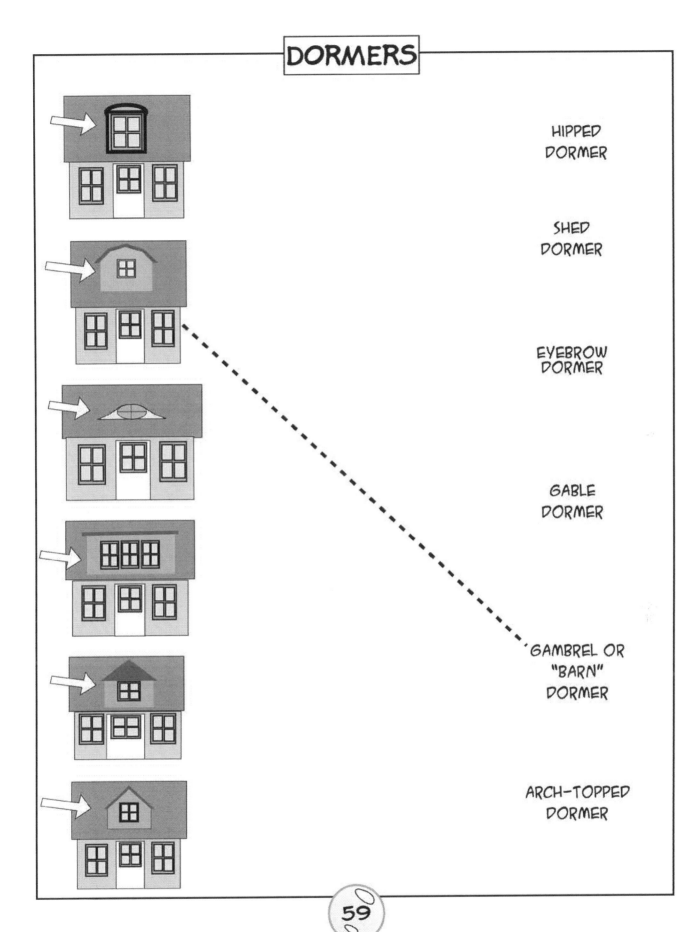

HIPPED
DORMER

SHED
DORMER

EYEBROW
DORMER

GABLE
DORMER

GAMBREL OR
"BARN"
DORMER

ARCH-TOPPED
DORMER

Consider This...

"THE FLOW THROUGH
ROOMS

THE MOVEMENT THROUGH THE
ROOMS IS AS IMPORTANT AS THE
ROOMS THEMSELVES."
A PATTERN LANGUAGE
CHRISTOPHER ALEXANDER @ 1977
P. 628

60

Floor Plan

WHICH WAY IS NORTH?

FLOOR PLAN: IF YOU ARE TRYING TO DESCRIBE THE WAY THE ROOMS IN A BUILDING ARE LAID OUT A FLOOR PLAN IS HELPFUL. A FLOOR PLAN IS A VIEW AS IF SEEN FROM ABOVE. WHEN SHOWING SYSTEMS LIKE PLUMBING AND ELECTRICAL A FLOOR PLAN IS USEFUL TOO.

If you are drawing a building and it looks like this →

ELEVATION

*YOU WOULD NOT ACTUALLY WRITE THESE WORDS ON THE FACE OF YOUR DRAWING. I PUT THEM ON THIS DRAWING TO SHOW YOU WHAT DIFFERENT ELEMENTS MIGHT LOOK LIKE SO YOU CAN DRAW THEM YOURSELF. (JUST DON'T LABEL THEM!)

The Floor Plan might look like this →

IF YOU ARE JUST INFORMALLY SKETCHING, AS YOU PROBABLY ARE IN THIS BOOK — YOU CAN SHOW WALLS AS LINES AND WINDOWS AS RECTANGLES THAT SIT ON THE WALLS.

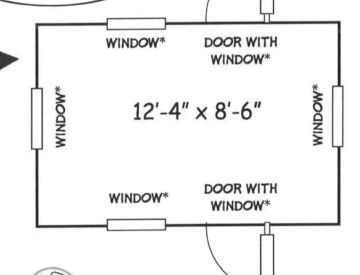

WINDOW*   DOOR WITH WINDOW*

WINDOW*   12'-4" x 8'-6"   WINDOW*

WINDOW*   DOOR WITH WINDOW*

THERE ARE DIFFERENT WAYS TO SHOW THE SIZE (DIMENSIONS) OF ROOMS. SOMETIMES THE DIMENSION MEASUREMENTS ARE PLACED INSIDE THE ROOMS.

If you are drawing a building and it looks like this

*YOU WOULD NOT ACTUALLY WRITE THESE WORDS ON THE FACE OF YOUR DRAWING. I PUT THEM ON THIS DRAWING TO SHOW YOU WHAT DIFFERENT ELEMENTS MIGHT LOOK LIKE SO YOU CAN DRAW THEM YOURSELF.

ELEVATION

IN THIS EXAMPLE DRAWING OF THE SAME BUILDING AS THE PRIOR PAGE, THE WALL THICKNESS IS SHOWN AND THE DIMENSIONS ARE SHOWN OUTSIDE THE DRAWING.

12'-4"

8'-6"

WINDOW*

DOOR WITH WINDOW*

WINDOW*

WINDOW*

WINDOW*

DOOR WITH WINDOW*

The Floor Plan might look like this

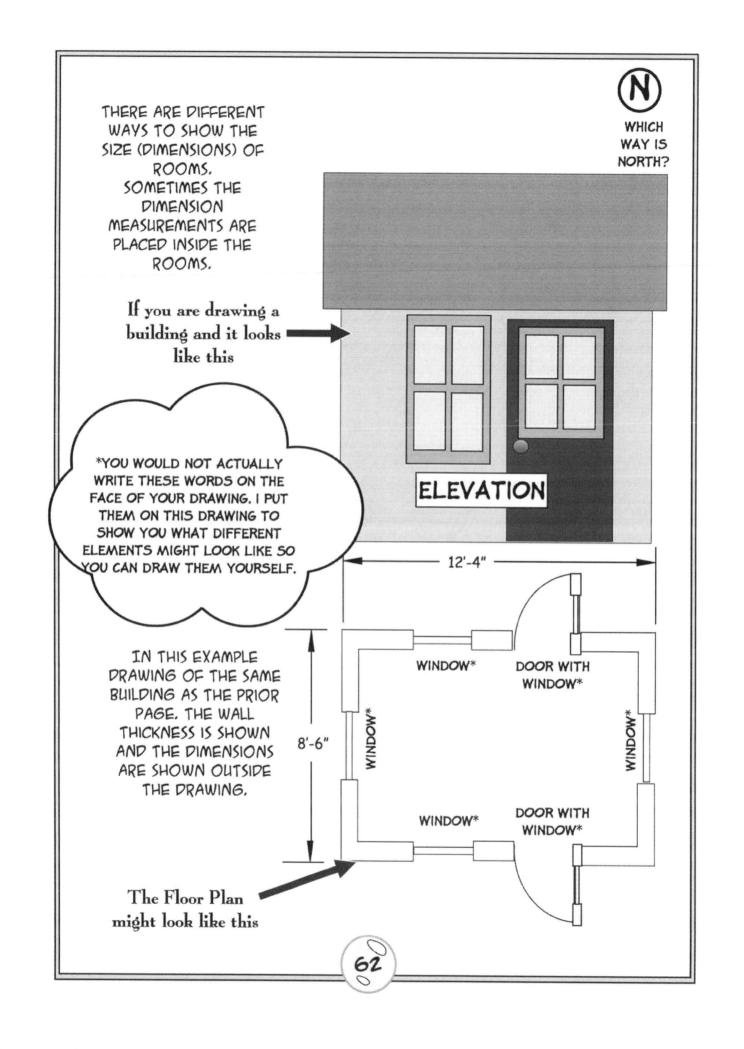

SOME FLOOR PLAN SYMBOLS

FIREPLACE

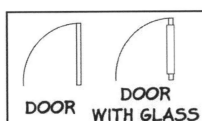

DOOR

DOOR WITH GLASS

FRENCH DOOR

CLOTHES IN CLOSET WITH SLIDING DOORS

KITCHEN TABLE AND CHAIRS

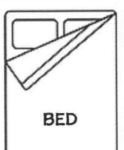

BED

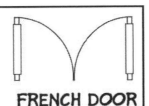

SOFA

CHAIR

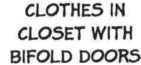

CLOTHES IN CLOSET WITH BIFOLD DOORS

SOME PLUMBING SYMBOLS

KITCHEN SINK

HW

HOT WATER HEATER

BATHROOM SINK

TOILET

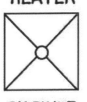

SHOWER

STAIR EXAMPLES

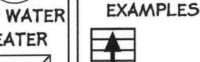

SOME ELECTRICAL SYMBOLS

SWITCH

2-WAY SWITCH

3-WAY SWITCH

SWITCH WITH DIMMER

110 VOLT DUPLEX OUTLET (2 SOCKETS)

GFI

RECEPTACLE WITH GROUND FAULT INTERRUPTER

110 VOLT FOURPLEX OUTLET (4 SOCKETS)

220

220 VOLT OUTLET

WALL-MOUNTED LIGHT

CIRCUIT BREAKER

TELEPHONE OR DATA JACK

SD

SMOKE DETECTOR

T

THERMOSTAT

SAMPLE
FLOOR PLAN

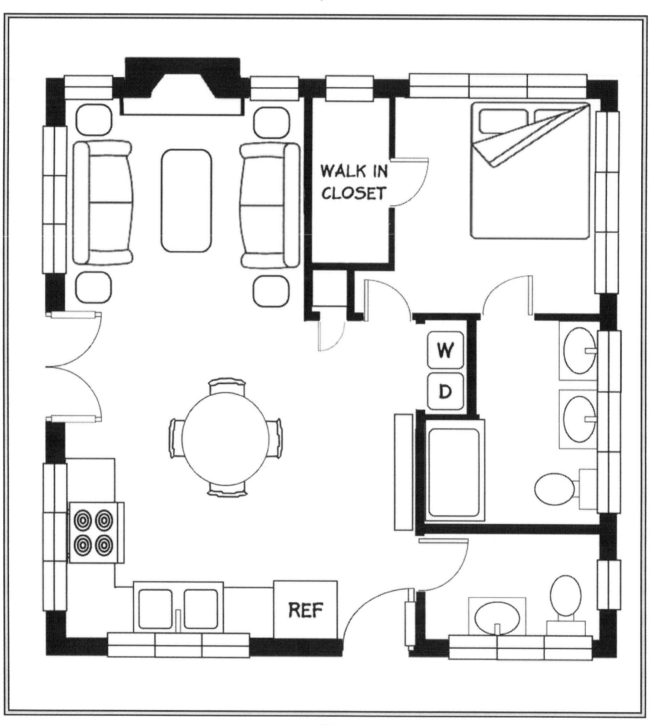

WALK IN
CLOSET

W

D

REF

Plot/Site Plan

This view of property shows how things look from above - a bird's eye view, or the view from an airplane. To be able to fit an entire yard or property on one page this is drawn to a different scale than an elevation or a floor plan.

For example a house is drawn much smaller so you can draw other buildings around it and trees and to give an idea of how things are laid out. Below are shown a few of the symbols you might find helpful. You can go online to look up other symbols if you are interested.

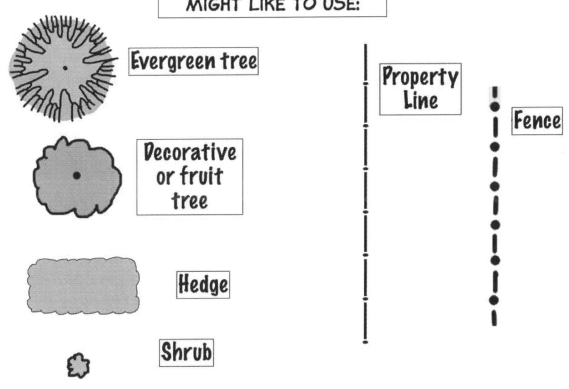

SOME SYMBOLS YOU MIGHT LIKE TO USE:

Evergreen tree

Decorative or fruit tree

Hedge

Shrub

Property Line

Fence

SOME PLOT/SITE PLAN ROOFS

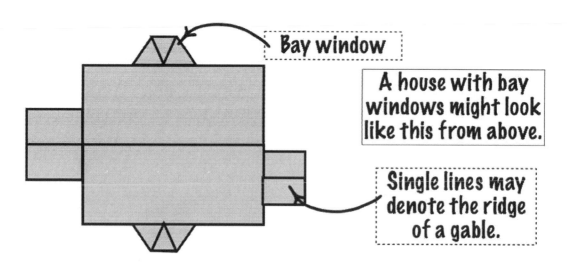

Bay window

A house with bay windows might look like this from above.

Single lines may denote the ridge of a gable.

If you were a bird looking down on a barn all you would probably see would be the roof.

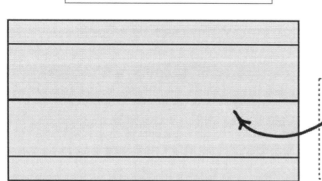

A barn with a gambrel/barn roof might be shown like this.

This single line through the middle could show the ridge of the roof.

IF YOU ARE LAYING OUT YOUR OWN PROPERTY YOU MIGHT WANT TO THINK ABOUT THESE THINGS:

Access to the house
Walks -- width, drainage, appearance, and lighting
Driveways -- type of surface and amount of turnaround space
Parking -- for family, guests, a camper, a boat, or bicycles

Family Activities
Outdoor entertaining -- cooking, seating, and patio access
Children's play area
Sports, recreation
Extra parking for boat or recreational vehicle

Maintenance
Do you do your own yard work?
Storage for garden equipment
Specific gardening interests (for example, growing vegetables, roses, herbs, fruit trees, or bulbs)

Don't forget space for:
Garbage cans
Clothesline
Dog pens
Firewood storage

An Example of a Plot/Site Plan

7 BLUEBIRD LANE
CHINA, MAINE
PLOT/SITE PLAN

The Purple Cow
Farm & Market

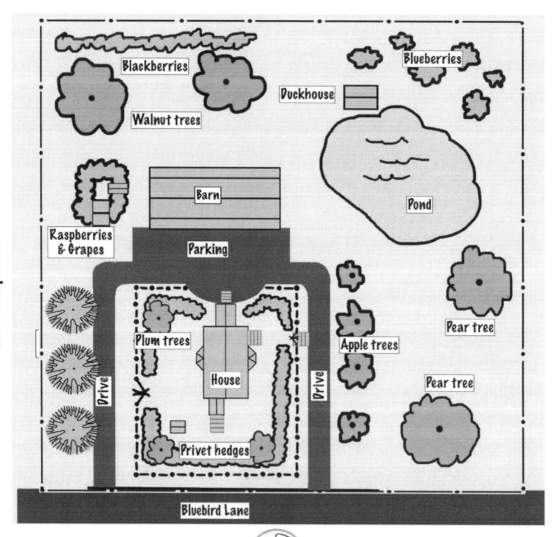

HOW TO

SKETCHING

AN EXPLANATION OF
THE SKETCH PAGES.

NOTE, THIS IS YOUR BOOK –
USE IT IN THE WAY THAT BEST SUITS YOU.
HAVE FUN!

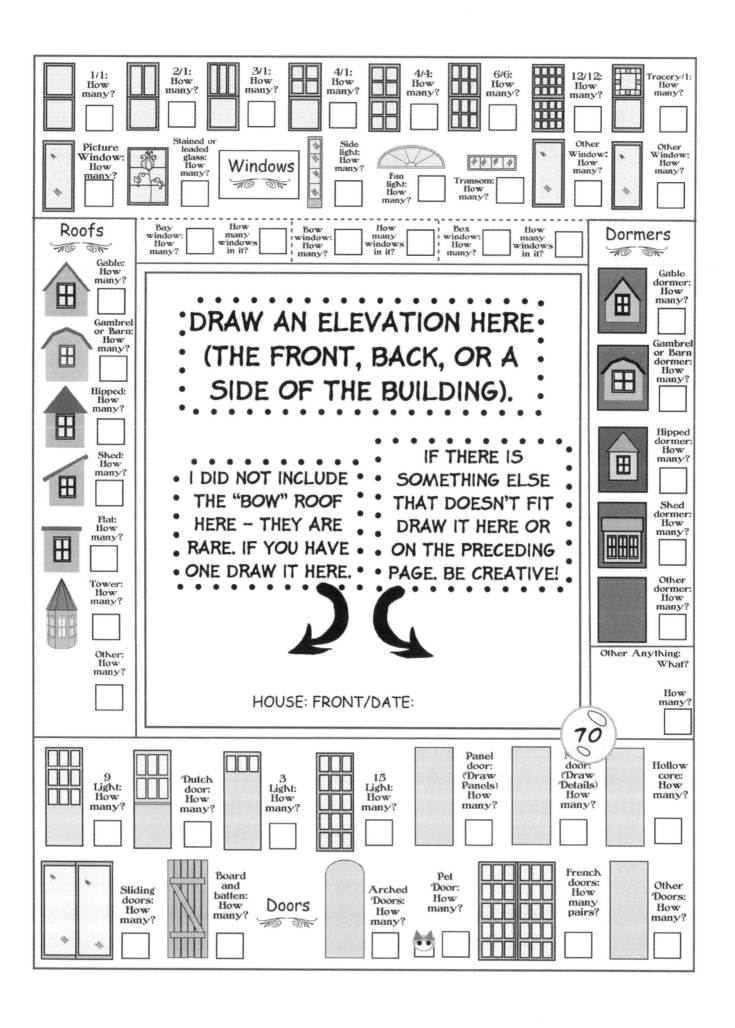

Windows

1/1: How many?

2/1: How many?

3/1: How many?

4/1: How many?

4/4: How many?

6/6: How many?

12/12: How many?

Tracery/1: How many?

Picture Window: How many?

Stained or leaded glass: How many?

Windows

Side light: How many?

Fan light: How many?

Transom: How many?

Other Window: How many?

Other Window: How many?

Bay window: How many?

How many windows in it?

Bow window: How many?

How many windows in it?

Box window: How many?

How many windows in it?

Roofs

Gable: How many?

Gambrel or Barn: How many?

Hipped: How many?

Shed: How many?

Flat: How many?

Tower: How many?

Other: How many?

Dormers

Gable dormer: How many?

Gambrel or Barn dormer: How many?

Hipped dormer: How many?

Shed dormer: How many?

Other dormer: How many?

Other Anything: What?

How many?

DRAW AN ELEVATION HERE (THE FRONT, BACK, OR A SIDE OF THE BUILDING).

I DID NOT INCLUDE THE "BOW" ROOF HERE – THEY ARE RARE. IF YOU HAVE ONE DRAW IT HERE.

IF THERE IS SOMETHING ELSE THAT DOESN'T FIT DRAW IT HERE OR ON THE PRECEDING PAGE. BE CREATIVE!

HOUSE: FRONT/DATE:

70

Doors

9 Light: How many?

Dutch door: How many?

3 Light: How many?

15 Light: How many?

Panel door: (Draw Panels) How many?

door: (Draw Details) How many?

Hollow core: How many?

Sliding doors: How many?

Board and batten: How many?

Doors

Arched Doors: How many?

Pet Door: How many?

French doors: How many pairs?

Other Doors: How many?

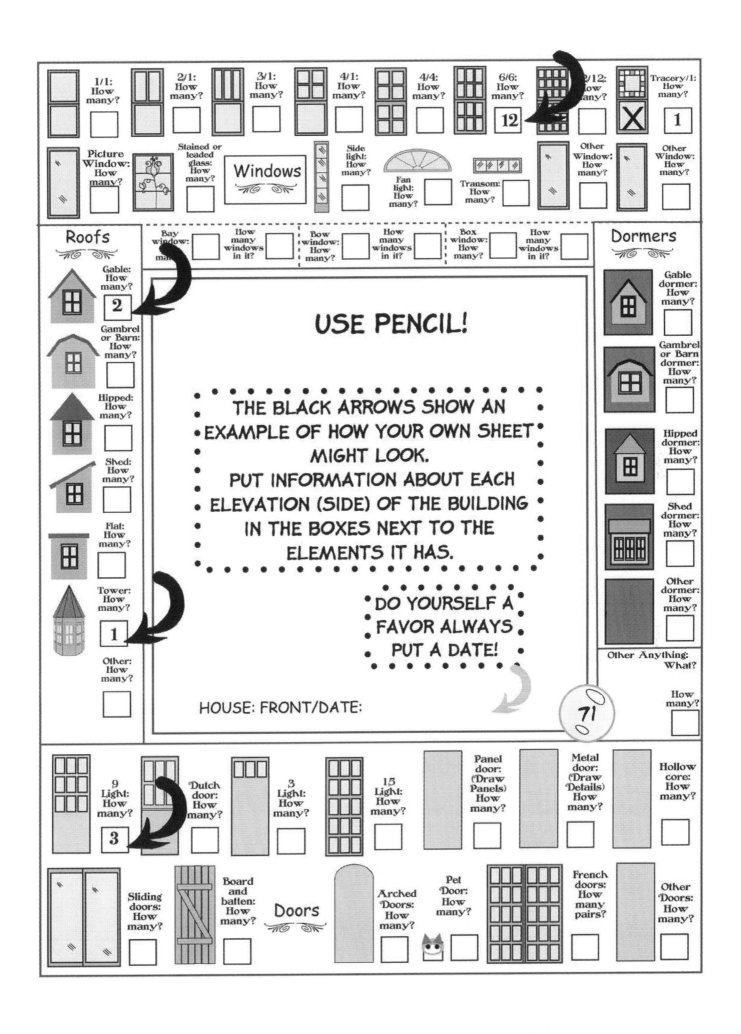

Windows

1/1: How many?
2/1: How many?
3/1: How many?
4/1: How many?
4/4: How many?
6/6: How many? 12
?/12: How many?
Tracery/1: How many? 1

Picture Window: How many?
Stained or leaded glass: How many?
Side light: How many?
Fan light: How many?
Transom: How many?
Other Window: How many?
Other Window: How many?

Bay window: How many? / How many windows in it?
Bow window: How many? / How many windows in it?
Box window: How many? / How many windows in it?

Roofs

Gable: How many? 2
Gambrel or Barn: How many?
Hipped: How many?
Shed: How many?
Flat: How many?
Tower: How many? 1
Other: How many?

USE PENCIL!

THE BLACK ARROWS SHOW AN EXAMPLE OF HOW YOUR OWN SHEET MIGHT LOOK.
PUT INFORMATION ABOUT EACH ELEVATION (SIDE) OF THE BUILDING IN THE BOXES NEXT TO THE ELEMENTS IT HAS.

DO YOURSELF A FAVOR ALWAYS PUT A DATE!

HOUSE: FRONT/DATE:

71

Dormers

Gable dormer: How many?
Gambrel or Barn dormer: How many?
Hipped dormer: How many?
Shed dormer: How many?
Other dormer: How many?
Other Anything: What? How many?

Doors

9 Light: How many? 3
Dutch door: How many?
3 Light: How many?
15 Light: How many?
Panel door: (Draw Panels) How many?
Metal door: (Draw Details) How many?
Hollow core: How many?
Sliding doors: How many?
Board and batten: How many?
Arched Doors: How many?
Pet Door: How many?
French doors: How many pairs?
Other Doors: How many?

UNUSUAL DOORS: DRAW THEM   UNUSUAL WINDOWS: DRAW THEM

EXAMPLE: FRONT

ROOF:

WHAT IS YOUR ROOF MADE OF?
Asphalt shingles

WHAT STICKS OUT OF YOUR ROOF:

CHIMNEYS?

YES ☑   NO ☐

HOW MANY CHIMNEYS?   3

WHAT ARE THE CHIMNEYS MADE OF?
2 made of bricks

1 made of metal

VENT STACK OR ELECTRIC LINES?

YES. ☑   NO ☐   (THESE LOOK LIKE PIPES.)

FOUNDATION:

WHAT KIND OF FOUNDATION
DOES YOUR HOUSE HAVE?

Brick-faced Stone

WHAT STICKS OUT OF YOUR
FOUNDATION?

Electric Line

Pipe to fill Oil Tank

Gas Line

Water Spigot

FLOOR PLAN FIRST FLOOR

WALK IN CLOSET

W

D

REF

(N) ↑ WHICH WAY IS NORTH?

How many rooms? **3**

HOUSE DATE:

Name the rooms and note what the ceiling, floor, and walls are made of.

#	NAME OF ROOM	CEILING	WALLS	FLOOR
1	Living	Plaster	Wood	Wood
2	Kitchen - eat in	Plaster	Wood	Tile
3	Bedroom	Plaster	Wood	Wood
4				
5				
6				
7				
8				

73

PLOT PLAN OF HOUSE

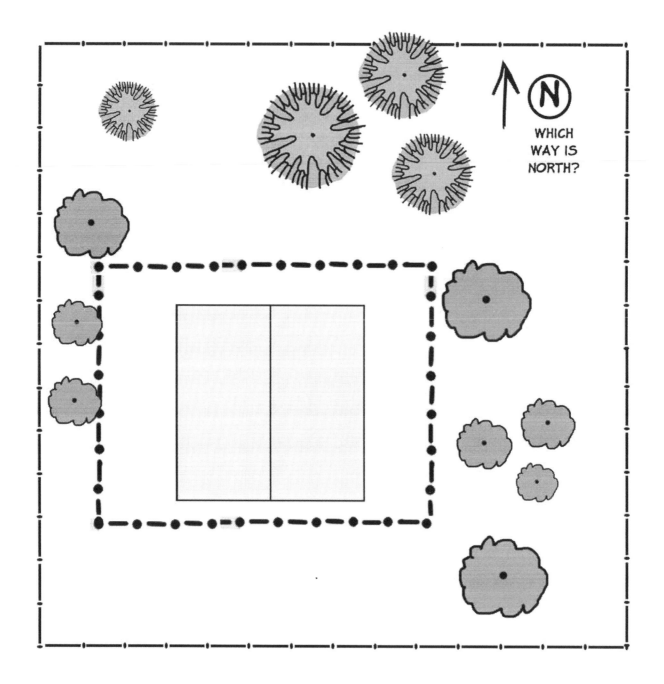

WHICH
WAY IS
NORTH?

12 Shadylane Avenue
Northboro, Maine

DATE: 25 December, 2012

WHEN DRAWING THE
OUTSIDE OF YOUR HOUSE
YOU MAY WANT TO
WORK LIKE THIS:

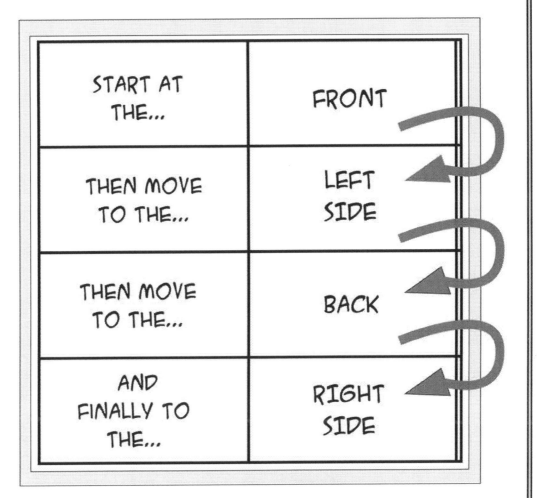

START AT THE...	FRONT
THEN MOVE TO THE...	LEFT SIDE
THEN MOVE TO THE...	BACK
AND FINALLY TO THE...	RIGHT SIDE

NOTE: I DIDN'T PUT THE FRONT RIGHT NEXT
TO THE BACK – BECAUSE AS YOU GO FROM
ONE TO ANOTHER – YOU'LL PASS EITHER THE
RIGHT OR LEFT SIDE AND YOU MIGHT AS
WELL DRAW THAT WHILE YOU'RE THERE.

If you're doing it right you'll look kind of like this.

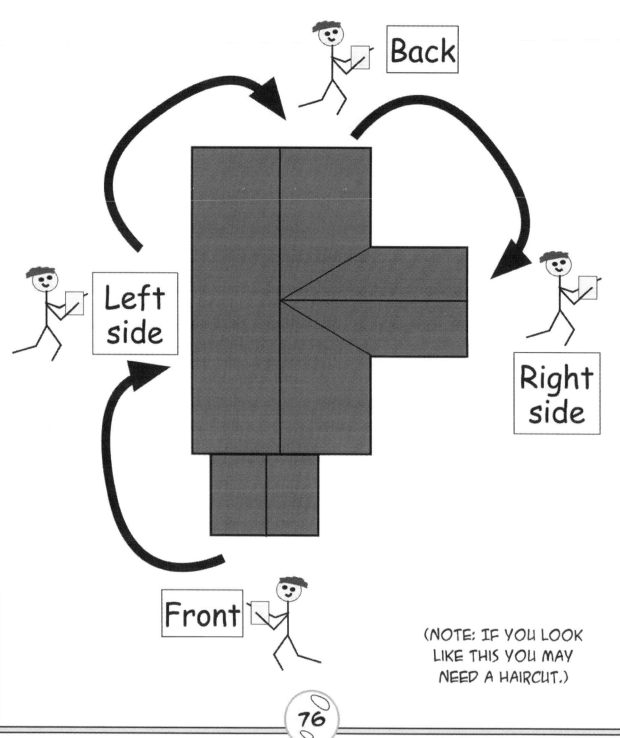

Back

Left side

Right side

Front

(NOTE: IF YOU LOOK LIKE THIS YOU MAY NEED A HAIRCUT.)

DATE: _____

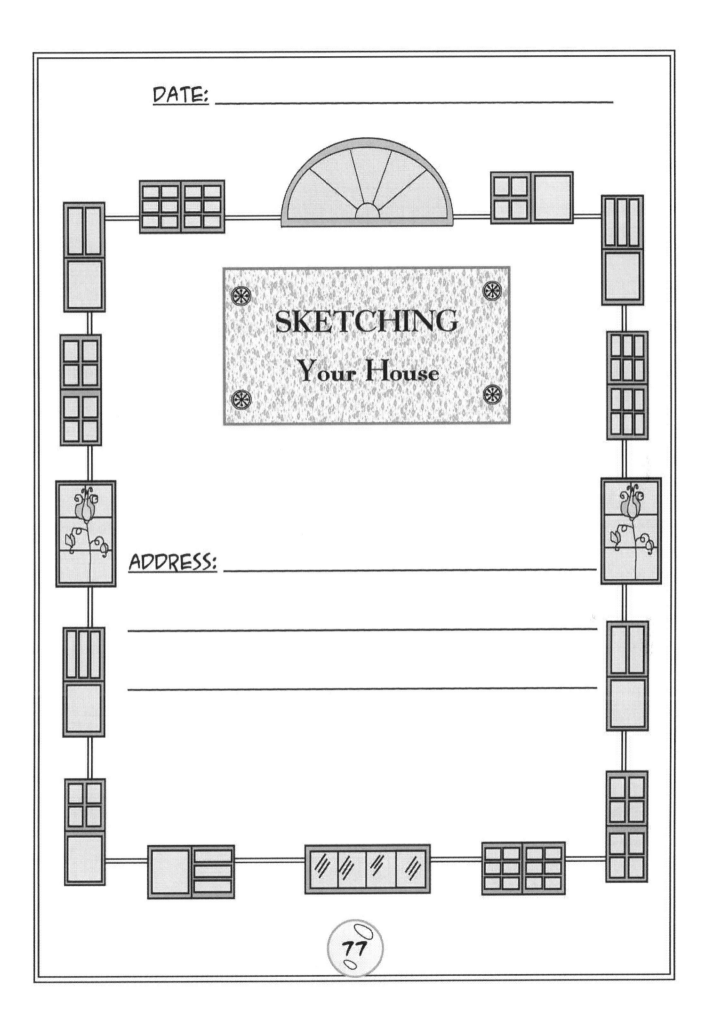

SKETCHING
Your House

ADDRESS: _____

_____

_____

UNUSUAL DOORS: DRAW THEM   UNUSUAL WINDOWS: DRAW THEM

HOUSE: FRONT

ROOF:

WHAT IS YOUR ROOF MADE OF?

_____

WHAT STICKS OUT OF YOUR ROOF:

CHIMNEYS?

YES ☐   NO ☐

HOW MANY CHIMNEYS? ☐

WHAT ARE THE CHIMNEYS MADE OF?

_____

_____

VENT STACK OR ELECTRIC LINES?

YES, ☐   NO ☐   (THESE LOOK LIKE PIPES.)

FOUNDATION:

WHAT KIND OF FOUNDATION DOES YOUR HOUSE HAVE?

_____

WHAT STICKS OUT OF YOUR FOUNDATION?

_____

_____

_____

_____

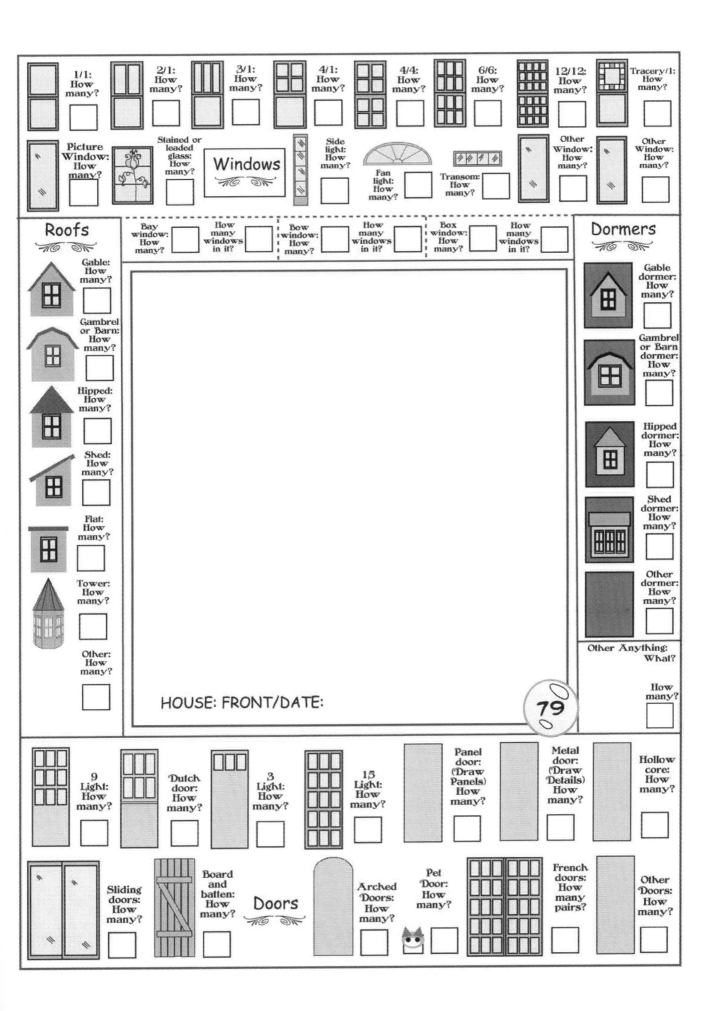

1/1: How many? ☐

2/1: How many? ☐

3/1: How many? ☐

4/1: How many? ☐

4/4: How many? ☐

6/6: How many? ☐

12/12: How many? ☐

Tracery/1: How many? ☐

Picture Window: How many? ☐

Stained or leaded glass: How many? ☐

Windows

Side light: How many? ☐

Fan light: How many? ☐

Transom: How many? ☐

Other Window: How many? ☐

Other Window: How many? ☐

Bay window: How many? ☐ How many windows in it? ☐

Bow window: How many? ☐ How many windows in it? ☐

Box window: How many? ☐ How many windows in it? ☐

Roofs

Gable: How many? ☐

Gambrel or Barn: How many? ☐

Hipped: How many? ☐

Shed: How many? ☐

Flat: How many? ☐

Tower: How many? ☐

Other: How many? ☐

Dormers

Gable dormer: How many? ☐

Gambrel or Barn dormer: How many? ☐

Hipped dormer: How many? ☐

Shed dormer: How many? ☐

Other dormer: How many? ☐

Other Anything: What?

How many? ☐

HOUSE: FRONT/DATE:

79

9 Light: How many? ☐

Dutch door: How many? ☐

3 Light: How many? ☐

15 Light: How many? ☐

Panel door: (Draw Panels) How many? ☐

Metal door: (Draw Details) How many? ☐

Hollow core: How many? ☐

Sliding doors: How many? ☐

Board and batten: How many? ☐

Doors

Arched Doors: How many? ☐

Pet Door: How many? ☐

French doors: How many pairs? ☐

Other Doors: How many? ☐

UNUSUAL DOORS: DRAW THEM   UNUSUAL WINDOWS: DRAW THEM

HOUSE: LEFT SIDE

ROOF: FOUNDATION:

WHAT IS YOUR ROOF MADE OF?   WHAT KIND OF FOUNDATION
                                   DOES YOUR HOUSE HAVE?
_____

WHAT STICKS OUT OF YOUR ROOF: _____

CHIMNEYS?

YES ☐   NO ☐   WHAT STICKS OUT OF YOUR
                                   FOUNDATION?
HOW MANY CHIMNEYS? ☐
                                   _____
WHAT ARE THE CHIMNEYS MADE OF?
                                   _____
_____
                                   _____
_____
                                   _____
VENT STACK OR ELECTRIC LINES?
                                   _____
YES, ☐   NO ☐   (THESE
                   LOOK LIKE
                   PIPES.)

80

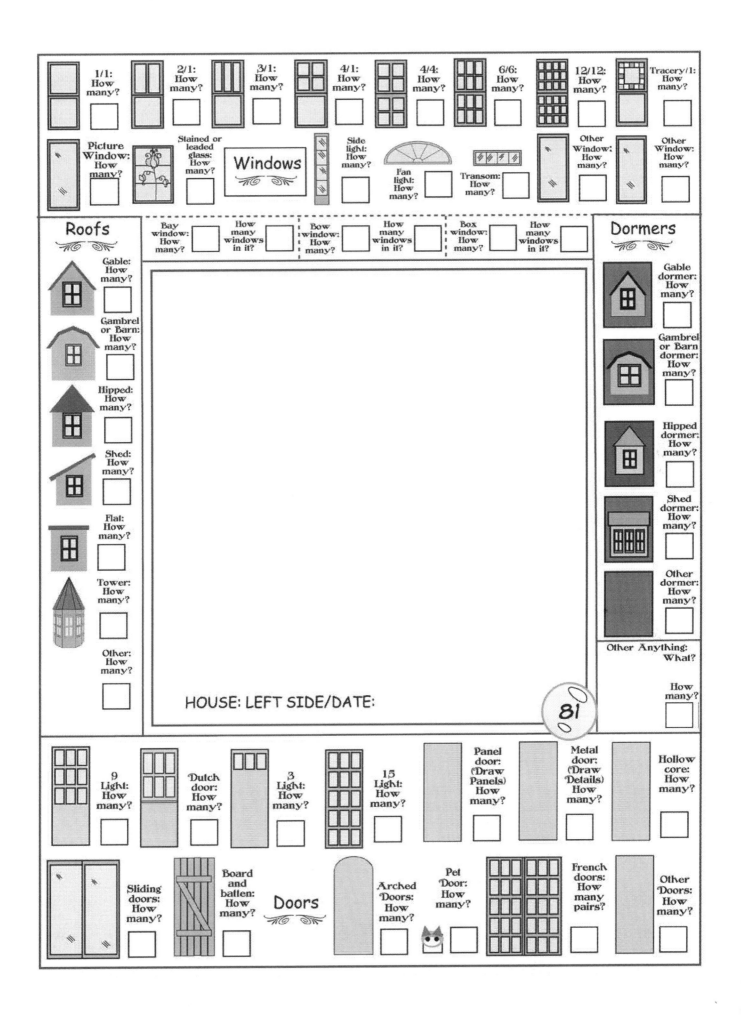

Windows

1/1: How many? ☐

2/1: How many? ☐

3/1: How many? ☐

4/1: How many? ☐

4/4: How many? ☐

6/6: How many? ☐

12/12: How many? ☐

Tracery/1: How many? ☐

Picture Window: How many? ☐

Stained or leaded glass: How many? ☐

Side light: How many? ☐

Fan light: How many? ☐

Transom: How many? ☐

Other Window: How many? ☐

Other Window: How many? ☐

Bay window: How many? ☐ How many windows in it? ☐

Bow window: How many? ☐ How many windows in it? ☐

Box window: How many? ☐ How many windows in it? ☐

Roofs

Gable: How many? ☐

Gambrel or Barn: How many? ☐

Hipped: How many? ☐

Shed: How many? ☐

Flat: How many? ☐

Tower: How many? ☐

Other: How many? ☐

Dormers

Gable dormer: How many? ☐

Gambrel or Barn dormer: How many? ☐

Hipped dormer: How many? ☐

Shed dormer: How many? ☐

Other dormer: How many? ☐

Other Anything: What? How many? ☐

HOUSE: LEFT SIDE/DATE:

81

Doors

9 Light: How many? ☐

Dutch door: How many? ☐

3 Light: How many? ☐

15 Light: How many? ☐

Panel door: (Draw Panels) How many? ☐

Metal door: (Draw Details) How many? ☐

Hollow core: How many? ☐

Sliding doors: How many? ☐

Board and batten: How many? ☐

Arched Doors: How many? ☐

Pet Door: How many? ☐

French doors: How many pairs? ☐

Other Doors: How many? ☐

UNUSUAL DOORS: DRAW THEM   UNUSUAL WINDOWS: DRAW THEM

HOUSE: BACK

ROOF: FOUNDATION:

WHAT IS YOUR ROOF MADE OF?   WHAT KIND OF FOUNDATION
                                   DOES YOUR HOUSE HAVE?
_____

WHAT STICKS OUT OF YOUR ROOF: _____

CHIMNEYS?

YES ☐   NO ☐   WHAT STICKS OUT OF YOUR
                                   FOUNDATION?
HOW MANY CHIMNEYS? ☐

WHAT ARE THE CHIMNEYS MADE OF?   _____

_____   _____

_____   _____

VENT STACK OR ELECTRIC LINES?   _____

YES, ☐   NO ☐   (THESE
                  LOOK LIKE
                  PIPES.)

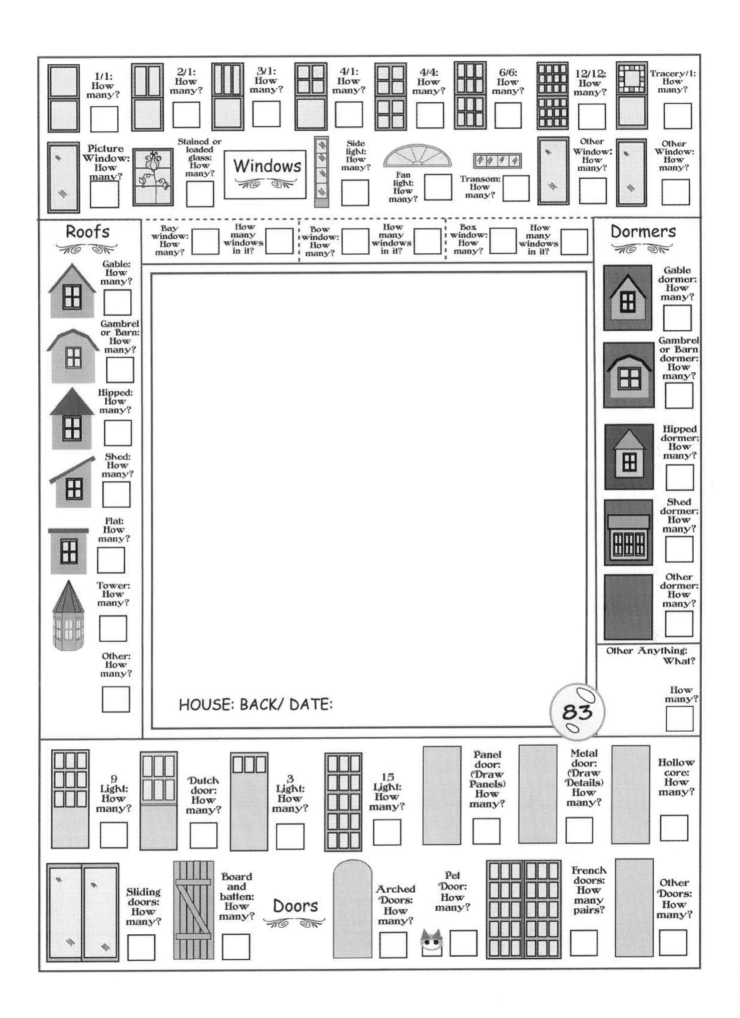

Windows

1/1: How many?
2/1: How many?
3/1: How many?
4/1: How many?
4/4: How many?
6/6: How many?
12/12: How many?
Tracery/1: How many?

Picture Window: How many?
Stained or leaded glass: How many?
Side light: How many?
Fan light: How many?
Transom: How many?
Other Window: How many?
Other Window: How many?

Bay window: How many?
How many windows in it?
Bow window: How many?
How many windows in it?
Box window: How many?
How many windows in it?

Roofs

Gable: How many?
Gambrel or Barn: How many?
Hipped: How many?
Shed: How many?
Flat: How many?
Tower: How many?
Other: How many?

Dormers

Gable dormer: How many?
Gambrel or Barn dormer: How many?
Hipped dormer: How many?
Shed dormer: How many?
Other dormer: How many?

Other Anything: What?
How many?

HOUSE: BACK/ DATE:

83

Doors

9 Light: How many?
Dutch door: How many?
3 Light: How many?
15 Light: How many?
Panel door: (Draw Panels) How many?
Metal door: (Draw Details) How many?
Hollow core: How many?

Sliding doors: How many?
Board and batten: How many?
Arched Doors: How many?
Pet Door: How many?
French doors: How many pairs?
Other Doors: How many?

UNUSUAL DOORS: DRAW THEM   UNUSUAL WINDOWS: DRAW THEM

HOUSE: RIGHT SIDE

ROOF:

WHAT IS YOUR ROOF MADE OF?

_____

WHAT STICKS OUT OF YOUR ROOF:

CHIMNEYS?

YES ☐   NO ☐

HOW MANY CHIMNEYS? ☐

WHAT ARE THE CHIMNEYS MADE OF?

_____

_____

VENT STACK OR ELECTRIC LINES?

YES. ☐   NO ☐   (THESE LOOK LIKE PIPES.)

FOUNDATION:

WHAT KIND OF FOUNDATION DOES YOUR HOUSE HAVE?

_____

WHAT STICKS OUT OF YOUR FOUNDATION?

_____

_____

_____

_____

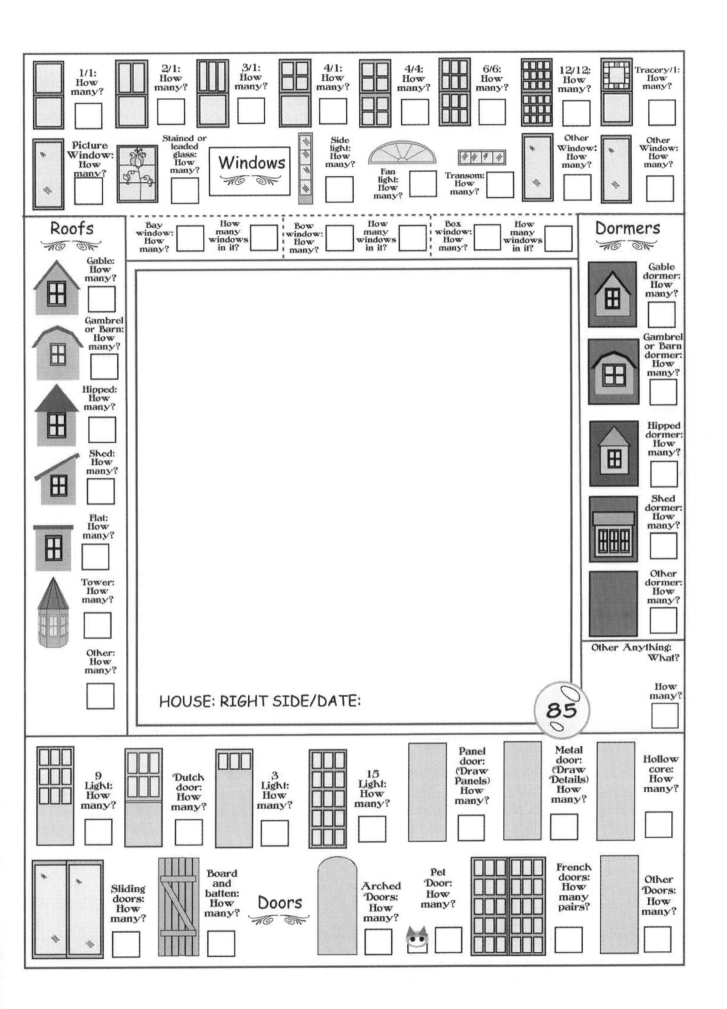

Windows

1/1: How many? ☐
2/1: How many? ☐
3/1: How many? ☐
4/1: How many? ☐
4/4: How many? ☐
6/6: How many? ☐
12/12: How many? ☐
Tracery/1: How many? ☐

Picture Window: How many? ☐
Stained or leaded glass: How many? ☐
Side light: How many? ☐
Fan light: How many? ☐
Transom: How many? ☐
Other Window: How many? ☐
Other Window: How many? ☐

Bay window: How many? ☐ How many windows in it? ☐
Bow window: How many? ☐ How many windows in it? ☐
Box window: How many? ☐ How many windows in it? ☐

Roofs

Gable: How many? ☐
Gambrel or Barn: How many? ☐
Hipped: How many? ☐
Shed: How many? ☐
Flat: How many? ☐
Tower: How many? ☐
Other: How many? ☐

HOUSE: RIGHT SIDE/DATE:

85

Dormers

Gable dormer: How many? ☐
Gambrel or Barn dormer: How many? ☐
Hipped dormer: How many? ☐
Shed dormer: How many? ☐
Other dormer: How many? ☐

Other Anything: What?

How many? ☐

Doors

9 Light: How many? ☐
Dutch door: How many? ☐
3 Light: How many? ☐
15 Light: How many? ☐
Panel door: (Draw Panels) How many? ☐
Metal door: (Draw Details) How many? ☐
Hollow core: How many? ☐

Sliding doors: How many? ☐
Board and batten: How many? ☐
Arched Doors: How many? ☐
Pet Door: How many? ☐
French doors: How many pairs? ☐
Other Doors: How many? ☐

FLOOR PLAN BASEMENT

How many rooms? ☐   HOUSE DATE:

Name the rooms and note what the ceiling, floor, and walls are made of.

#	NAME OF ROOM	CEILING	WALLS	FLOOR
1				
2				
3				
4				
5				
6				
7				
8				

FLOOR PLAN FIRST FLOOR

WHICH
WAY IS
NORTH?

How many rooms? ☐   HOUSE DATE:

Name the rooms and note what the ceiling, floor, and walls are made of.

#	NAME OF ROOM	CEILING	WALLS	FLOOR
1				
2				
3				
4				
5				
6				
7				
8				

FLOOR PLAN SECOND FLOOR

(N) WHICH WAY IS NORTH?

How many rooms? [ ]

HOUSE DATE:

Name the rooms and note what the ceiling, floor, and walls are made of.

#	NAME OF ROOM	CEILING	WALLS	FLOOR
1				
2				
3				
4				
5				
6				
7				
8				

88

FLOOR PLAN THIRD FLOOR

WHICH
WAY IS
NORTH?

How many rooms? ☐   HOUSE DATE:

Name the rooms and note what the ceiling, floor, and walls are made of.

#	NAME OF ROOM	CEILING	WALLS	FLOOR
1				
2				
3				
4				
5				
6				
7				
8				

FLOOR PLAN FOURTH FLOOR

N

WHICH WAY IS NORTH?

How many rooms? ☐

HOUSE DATE:

Name the rooms and note what the ceiling, floor, and walls are made of.

#	NAME OF ROOM	CEILING	WALLS	FLOOR
1				
2				
3				
4				
5				
6				
7				
8				

90

FLOOR PLAN ATTIC

WHICH
WAY IS
NORTH?

How many rooms? ☐   HOUSE DATE:

Name the rooms and note what the ceiling, floor, and walls are made of.

#	NAME OF ROOM	CEILING	WALLS	FLOOR
1				
2				
3				
4				
5				
6				
7				
8				

PLOT PLAN OF HOUSE

WHICH
WAY IS
NORTH?

DATE:

DATE: _____

SKETCHING

Building #2

NAME OF BUILDING: _____

ADDRESS: _____

_____

_____

UNUSUAL DOORS: DRAW THEM   UNUSUAL WINDOWS: DRAW THEM

BUILDING #2: FRONT

ROOF: FOUNDATION:

WHAT IS YOUR ROOF MADE OF?   WHAT KIND OF FOUNDATION
                                        DOES YOUR HOUSE HAVE?
_____

WHAT STICKS OUT OF YOUR ROOF: _____

CHIMNEYS?

YES ☐   NO ☐   WHAT STICKS OUT OF YOUR
                                        FOUNDATION?
HOW MANY CHIMNEYS? ☐
                                        _____
WHAT ARE THE CHIMNEYS MADE OF?

_____   _____

_____   _____

VENT STACK OR ELECTRIC LINES?   _____

YES, ☐   NO ☐   (THESE
                 LOOK LIKE
                 PIPES.)

94

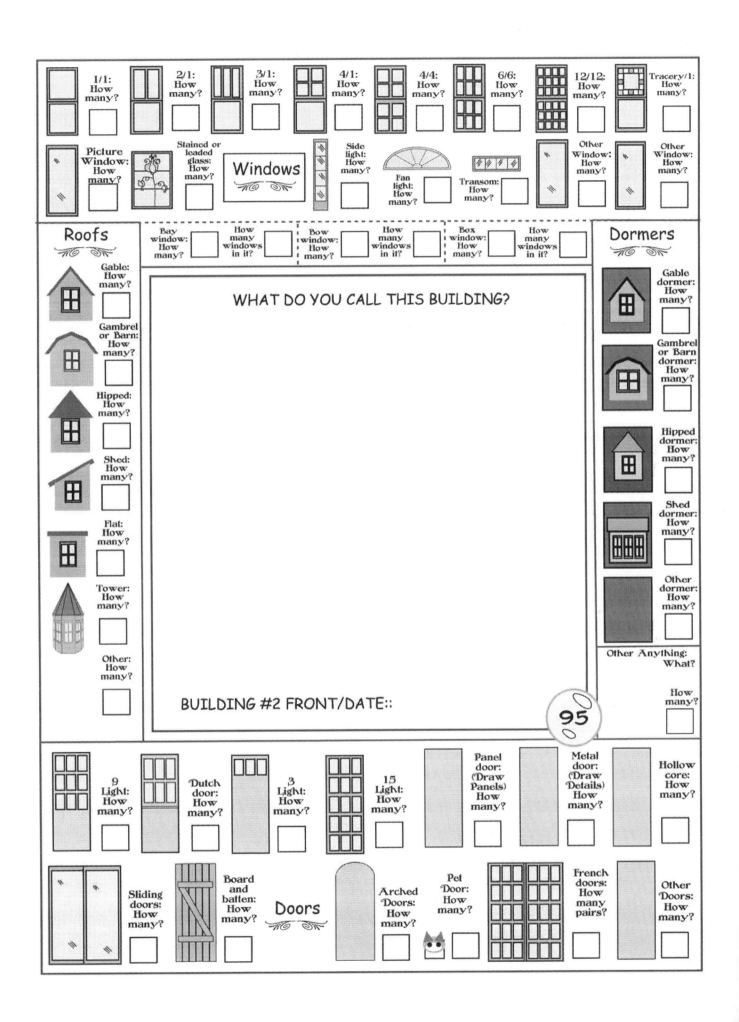

Windows

1/1: How many?

2/1: How many?

3/1: How many?

4/1: How many?

4/4: How many?

6/6: How many?

12/12: How many?

Tracery/1: How many?

Picture Window: How many?

Stained or leaded glass: How many?

Side light: How many?

Fan light: How many?

Transom: How many?

Other Window: How many?

Other Window: How many?

Roofs

Gable: How many?

Gambrel or Barn: How many?

Hipped: How many?

Shed: How many?

Flat: How many?

Tower: How many?

Other: How many?

Bay window: How many?

How many windows in it?

Bow window: How many?

How many windows in it?

Box window: How many?

How many windows in it?

WHAT DO YOU CALL THIS BUILDING?

BUILDING #2 FRONT/DATE::

95

Dormers

Gable dormer: How many?

Gambrel or Barn dormer: How many?

Hipped dormer: How many?

Shed dormer: How many?

Other dormer: How many?

Other Anything: What?

How many?

9 Light: How many?

Dutch door: How many?

3 Light: How many?

15 Light: How many?

Panel door: (Draw Panels) How many?

Metal door: (Draw Details) How many?

Hollow core: How many?

Sliding doors: How many?

Board and batten: How many?

Doors

Arched Doors: How many?

Pet Door: How many?

French doors: How many pairs?

Other Doors: How many?

UNUSUAL DOORS: DRAW THEM UNUSUAL WINDOWS: DRAW THEM

BUILDING #2: LEFT SIDE

ROOF:

WHAT IS YOUR ROOF MADE OF?

_____

WHAT STICKS OUT OF YOUR ROOF:

CHIMNEYS?

YES ☐ NO ☐

HOW MANY CHIMNEYS? ☐

WHAT ARE THE CHIMNEYS MADE OF?

_____

_____

VENT STACK OR ELECTRIC LINES?

YES, ☐ NO ☐ (THESE
LOOK LIKE
PIPES.)

FOUNDATION:

WHAT KIND OF FOUNDATION
DOES YOUR HOUSE HAVE?

_____

WHAT STICKS OUT OF YOUR
FOUNDATION?

_____

_____

_____

_____

Windows

1/1: How many? ☐
2/1: How many? ☐
3/1: How many? ☐
4/1: How many? ☐
4/4: How many? ☐
6/6: How many? ☐
12/12: How many? ☐
Tracery/1: How many? ☐

Picture Window: How many? ☐
Stained or leaded glass: How many? ☐
Side light: How many? ☐
Fan light: How many? ☐
Transom: How many? ☐
Other Window: How many? ☐
Other Window: How many? ☐

Bay window: How many? ☐ How many windows in it? ☐
Bow window: How many? ☐ How many windows in it? ☐
Box window: How many? ☐ How many windows in it? ☐

Roofs

Gable: How many? ☐
Gambrel or Barn: How many? ☐
Hipped: How many? ☐
Shed: How many? ☐
Flat: How many? ☐
Tower: How many? ☐
Other: How many? ☐

WHAT DO YOU CALL THIS BUILDING?

BUILDING #2 LEFT SIDE:/DATE::

Dormers

Gable dormer: How many? ☐
Gambrel or Barn dormer: How many? ☐
Hipped dormer: How many? ☐
Shed dormer: How many? ☐
Other dormer: How many? ☐

Other Anything: What?
How many? ☐

97

Doors

9 Light: How many? ☐
Dutch door: How many? ☐
3 Light: How many? ☐
15 Light: How many? ☐
Panel door: (Draw Panels) How many? ☐
Metal door: (Draw Details) How many? ☐
Hollow core: How many? ☐

Sliding doors: How many? ☐
Board and batten: How many? ☐
Arched Doors: How many? ☐
Pet Door: How many? ☐
French doors: How many pairs? ☐
Other Doors: How many? ☐

UNUSUAL DOORS: DRAW THEM   UNUSUAL WINDOWS: DRAW THEM

BUILDING #2: BACK

ROOF: FOUNDATION:

WHAT IS YOUR ROOF MADE OF?   WHAT KIND OF FOUNDATION
                                   DOES YOUR HOUSE HAVE?
_____

WHAT STICKS OUT OF YOUR ROOF: _____

CHIMNEYS?

YES ☐   NO ☐   WHAT STICKS OUT OF YOUR
                                   FOUNDATION?
HOW MANY CHIMNEYS? ☐

WHAT ARE THE CHIMNEYS MADE OF?   _____

                                   _____
_____

                                   _____
_____

                                   _____
VENT STACK OR ELECTRIC LINES?

YES, ☐   NO ☐   (THESE
                LOOK LIKE
                PIPES.)

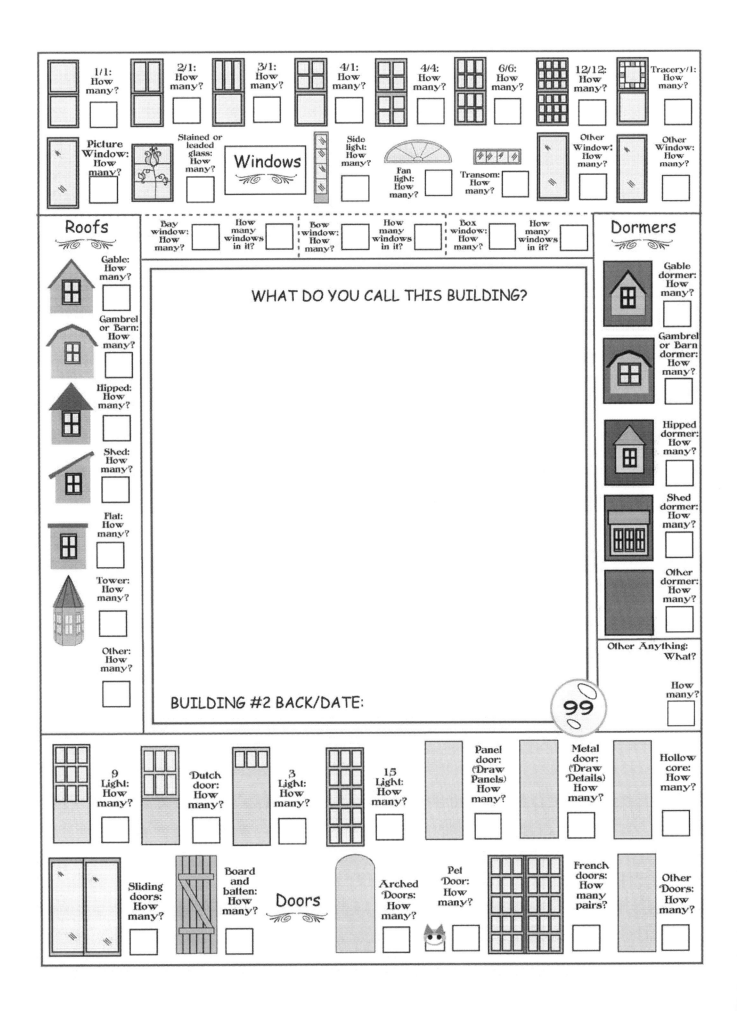

Windows

1/1: How many?

2/1: How many?

3/1: How many?

4/1: How many?

4/4: How many?

6/6: How many?

12/12: How many?

Tracery/1: How many?

Picture Window: How many?

Stained or leaded glass: How many?

Side light: How many?

Fan light: How many?

Transom: How many?

Other Window: How many?

Other Window: How many?

Bay window: How many?

How many windows in it?

Bow window: How many?

How many windows in it?

Box window: How many?

How many windows in it?

Roofs

Gable: How many?

Gambrel or Barn: How many?

Hipped: How many?

Shed: How many?

Flat: How many?

Tower: How many?

Other: How many?

Dormers

Gable dormer: How many?

Gambrel or Barn dormer: How many?

Hipped dormer: How many?

Shed dormer: How many?

Other dormer: How many?

Other Anything: What?

How many?

WHAT DO YOU CALL THIS BUILDING?

BUILDING #2 BACK/DATE:

99

Doors

9 Light: How many?

Dutch door: How many?

3 Light: How many?

15 Light: How many?

Panel door: (Draw Panels) How many?

Metal door: (Draw Details) How many?

Hollow core: How many?

Sliding doors: How many?

Board and batten: How many?

Arched Doors: How many?

Pet Door: How many?

French doors: How many pairs?

Other Doors: How many?

UNUSUAL DOORS: DRAW THEM   UNUSUAL WINDOWS: DRAW THEM

BUILDING #2: RIGHT SIDE

ROOF: FOUNDATION:

WHAT IS YOUR ROOF MADE OF?   WHAT KIND OF FOUNDATION
                                           DOES YOUR HOUSE HAVE?
_____

WHAT STICKS OUT OF YOUR ROOF:

CHIMNEYS?   _____

YES ☐   NO ☐   WHAT STICKS OUT OF YOUR
                                           FOUNDATION?
HOW MANY CHIMNEYS? ☐

WHAT ARE THE CHIMNEYS MADE OF?   _____

_____   _____

_____   _____

VENT STACK OR ELECTRIC LINES?   _____

YES, ☐   NO ☐   (THESE
                 LOOK LIKE
                 PIPES.)

100

Windows

1/1: How many? ☐
2/1: How many? ☐
3/1: How many? ☐
4/1: How many? ☐
4/4: How many? ☐
6/6: How many? ☐
12/12: How many? ☐
Tracery/1: How many? ☐

Picture Window: How many? ☐
Stained or leaded glass: How many? ☐
Side light: How many? ☐
Fan light: How many? ☐
Transom: How many? ☐
Other Window: How many? ☐
Other Window: How many? ☐

Bay window: How many? ☐ How many windows in it? ☐
Bow window: How many? ☐ How many windows in it? ☐
Box window: How many? ☐ How many windows in it? ☐

Roofs

Gable: How many? ☐
Gambrel or Barn: How many? ☐
Hipped: How many? ☐
Shed: How many? ☐
Flat: How many? ☐
Tower: How many? ☐
Other: How many? ☐

Dormers

Gable dormer: How many? ☐
Gambrel or Barn dormer: How many? ☐
Hipped dormer: How many? ☐
Shed dormer: How many? ☐
Other dormer: How many? ☐

Other Anything: What?
How many? ☐

WHAT DO YOU CALL THIS BUILDING?

BUILDING #2 RIGHT SIDE/DATE:

101

Doors

9 Light: How many? ☐
Dutch door: How many? ☐
3 Light: How many? ☐
15 Light: How many? ☐
Panel door: (Draw Panels) How many? ☐
Metal door: (Draw Details) How many? ☐
Hollow core: How many? ☐

Sliding doors: How many? ☐
Board and batten: How many? ☐
Arched Doors: How many? ☐
Pet Door: How many? ☐
French doors: How many pairs? ☐
Other Doors: How many? ☐

FLOOR PLAN BASEMENT

WHICH
WAY IS
NORTH?

BUILDING #2

NAME OF BUILDING:

DATE:

How many rooms?

Name the rooms and note what the ceiling, floor, and walls are made of.

#	NAME OF ROOM	CEILING	WALLS	FLOOR
1				
2				
3				
4				
5				
6				
7				
8				

FLOOR PLAN FIRST FLOOR

WHICH
WAY IS
NORTH?

BUILDING #2

NAME OF BUILDING:

How many rooms? ☐

DATE:

Name the rooms and note what the ceiling, floor, and walls are made of.

#	NAME OF ROOM	CEILING	WALLS	FLOOR
1				
2				
3				
4				
5				
6				
7				
8				

103

FLOOR PLAN SECOND FLOOR

WHICH
WAY IS
NORTH?

BUILDING #2

NAME OF BUILDING:

How many rooms? ☐

DATE:

Name the rooms and note what the ceiling, floor, and walls are made of.

#	NAME OF ROOM	CEILING	WALLS	FLOOR
1				
2				
3				
4				
5				
6				
7				
8				

FLOOR PLAN THIRD FLOOR

WHICH WAY IS NORTH?

BUILDING #2

NAME OF BUILDING:

DATE:

How many rooms? ☐

Name the rooms and note what the ceiling, floor, and walls are made of.

#	NAME OF ROOM	CEILING	WALLS	FLOOR
1				
2				
3				
4				
5				
6				
7				
8				

FLOOR PLAN FOURTH FLOOR

WHICH
WAY IS
NORTH?

BUILDING #2

NAME OF BUILDING:

DATE:

How many rooms?

Name the rooms and note what the ceiling, floor, and walls are made of.

#	NAME OF ROOM	CEILING	WALLS	FLOOR
1				
2				
3				
4				
5				
6				
7				
8				

FLOOR PLAN ATTIC

WHICH
WAY IS
NORTH?

BUILDING #2

NAME OF BUILDING:

How many rooms? ☐

DATE:

Name the rooms and note what the ceiling, floor, and walls are made of.

#	NAME OF ROOM	CEILING	WALLS	FLOOR
1				
2				
3				
4				
5				
6				
7				
8				

PLOT PLAN BUILDING #2
NAME OF BUILDING:

WHICH
WAY IS
NORTH?

DATE:

DATE: _____

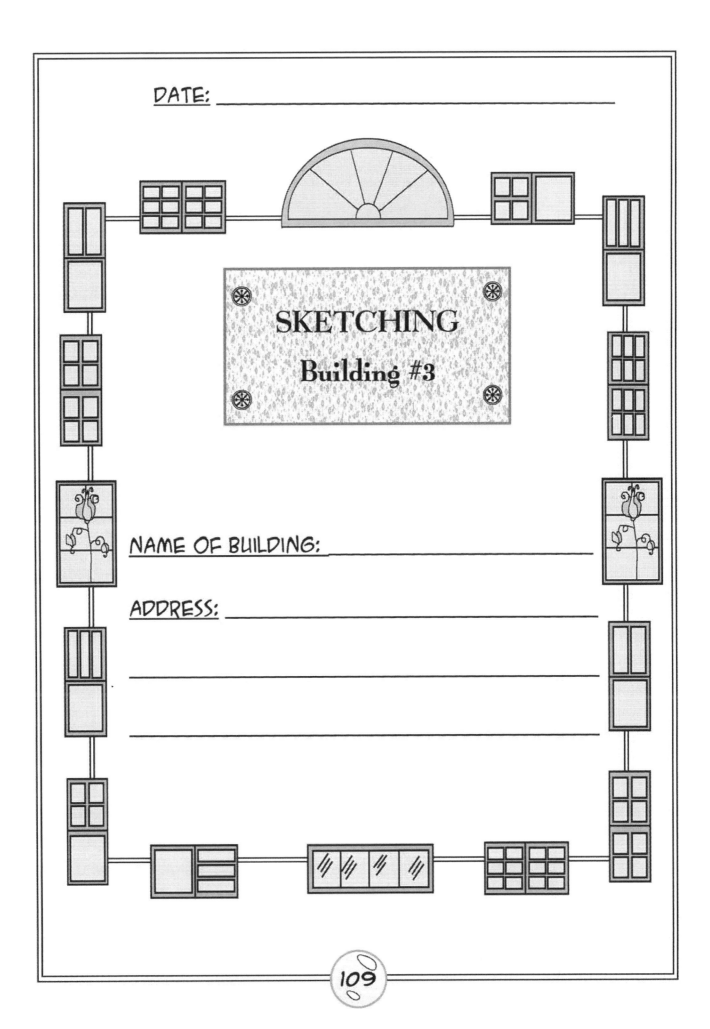

SKETCHING
Building #3

NAME OF BUILDING: _____

ADDRESS: _____

_____

_____

UNUSUAL DOORS: DRAW THEM   UNUSUAL WINDOWS: DRAW THEM

BUILDING #3: FRONT

ROOF: FOUNDATION:

WHAT IS YOUR ROOF MADE OF?   WHAT KIND OF FOUNDATION
                                         DOES YOUR HOUSE HAVE?
_____

WHAT STICKS OUT OF YOUR ROOF:

CHIMNEYS?   _____

YES ☐   NO ☐
                                         WHAT STICKS OUT OF YOUR
HOW MANY CHIMNEYS? ☐   FOUNDATION?

WHAT ARE THE CHIMNEYS MADE OF?   _____

_____   _____

_____   _____

VENT STACK OR ELECTRIC LINES?   _____

YES. ☐   NO ☐   (THESE
                 LOOK LIKE
                 PIPES.)

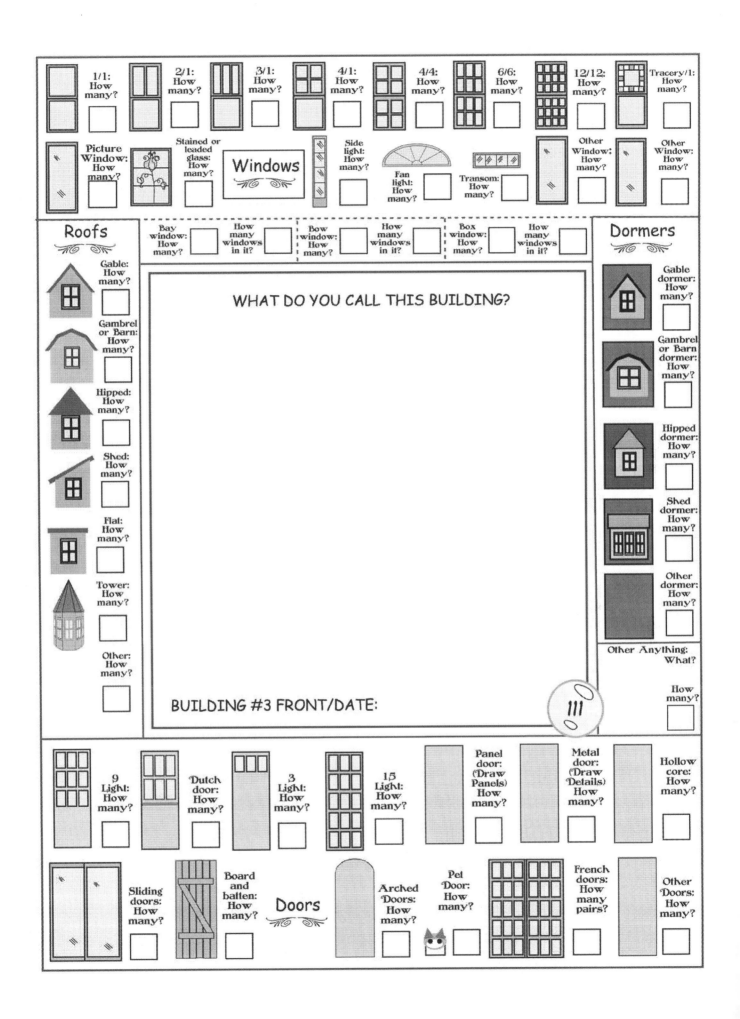

Windows

1/1: How many?
2/1: How many?
3/1: How many?
4/1: How many?
4/4: How many?
6/6: How many?
12/12: How many?
Tracery/1: How many?

Picture Window: How many?
Stained or leaded glass: How many?
Side light: How many?
Fan light: How many?
Transom: How many?
Other Window: How many?
Other Window: How many?

Bay window: How many?
How many windows in it?
Bow window: How many?
How many windows in it?
Box window: How many?
How many windows in it?

Roofs

Gable: How many?
Gambrel or Barn: How many?
Hipped: How many?
Shed: How many?
Flat: How many?
Tower: How many?
Other: How many?

WHAT DO YOU CALL THIS BUILDING?

BUILDING #3 FRONT/DATE:

111

Dormers

Gable dormer: How many?
Gambrel or Barn dormer: How many?
Hipped dormer: How many?
Shed dormer: How many?
Other dormer: How many?

Other Anything: What?

How many?

Doors

9 Light: How many?
Dutch door: How many?
3 Light: How many?
15 Light: How many?
Panel door: (Draw Panels) How many?
Metal door: (Draw Details) How many?
Hollow core: How many?

Sliding doors: How many?
Board and batten: How many?
Arched Doors: How many?
Pet Door: How many?
French doors: How many pairs?
Other Doors: How many?

UNUSUAL DOORS: DRAW THEM   UNUSUAL WINDOWS: DRAW THEM

BUILDING #3: LEFT SIDE

ROOF:

WHAT IS YOUR ROOF MADE OF?

_____

WHAT STICKS OUT OF YOUR ROOF:

CHIMNEYS?

YES [ ]   NO [ ]

HOW MANY CHIMNEYS? [ ]

WHAT ARE THE CHIMNEYS MADE OF?

_____

_____

VENT STACK OR ELECTRIC LINES?

YES, [ ]   NO [ ]   (THESE LOOK LIKE PIPES.)

FOUNDATION:

WHAT KIND OF FOUNDATION DOES YOUR HOUSE HAVE?

_____

WHAT STICKS OUT OF YOUR FOUNDATION?

_____

_____

_____

_____

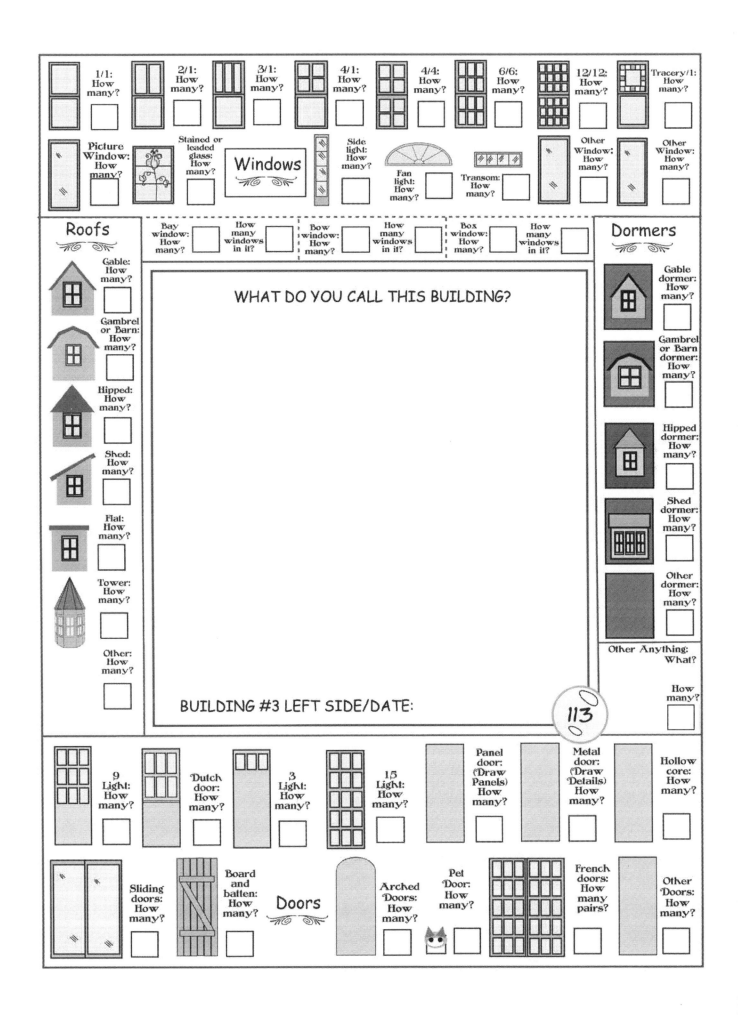

Windows

1/1: How many?

2/1: How many?

3/1: How many?

4/1: How many?

4/4: How many?

6/6: How many?

12/12: How many?

Tracery/1: How many?

Picture Window: How many?

Stained or leaded glass: How many?

Side light: How many?

Fan light: How many?

Transom: How many?

Other Window: How many?

Other Window: How many?

Bay window: How many?

How many windows in it?

Bow window: How many?

How many windows in it?

Box window: How many?

How many windows in it?

Roofs

Gable: How many?

Gambrel or Barn: How many?

Hipped: How many?

Shed: How many?

Flat: How many?

Tower: How many?

Other: How many?

Dormers

Gable dormer: How many?

Gambrel or Barn dormer: How many?

Hipped dormer: How many?

Shed dormer: How many?

Other dormer: How many?

Other Anything: What?

How many?

WHAT DO YOU CALL THIS BUILDING?

BUILDING #3 LEFT SIDE/DATE:

113

Doors

9 Light: How many?

Dutch door: How many?

3 Light: How many?

15 Light: How many?

Panel door: (Draw Panels) How many?

Metal door: (Draw Details) How many?

Hollow core: How many?

Sliding doors: How many?

Board and batten: How many?

Arched Doors: How many?

Pet Door: How many?

French doors: How many pairs?

Other Doors: How many?

UNUSUAL DOORS: DRAW THEM   UNUSUAL WINDOWS: DRAW THEM

BUILDING #3: BACK

ROOF: FOUNDATION:

WHAT IS YOUR ROOF MADE OF?   WHAT KIND OF FOUNDATION
                                   DOES YOUR HOUSE HAVE?
_____

WHAT STICKS OUT OF YOUR ROOF: _____

CHIMNEYS?
                                   WHAT STICKS OUT OF YOUR
YES ☐   NO ☐   FOUNDATION?

HOW MANY CHIMNEYS? ☐   _____

WHAT ARE THE CHIMNEYS MADE OF?   _____

_____   _____

_____   _____

VENT STACK OR ELECTRIC LINES?   _____

YES. ☐   NO ☐   (THESE
                  LOOK LIKE
                  PIPES.)

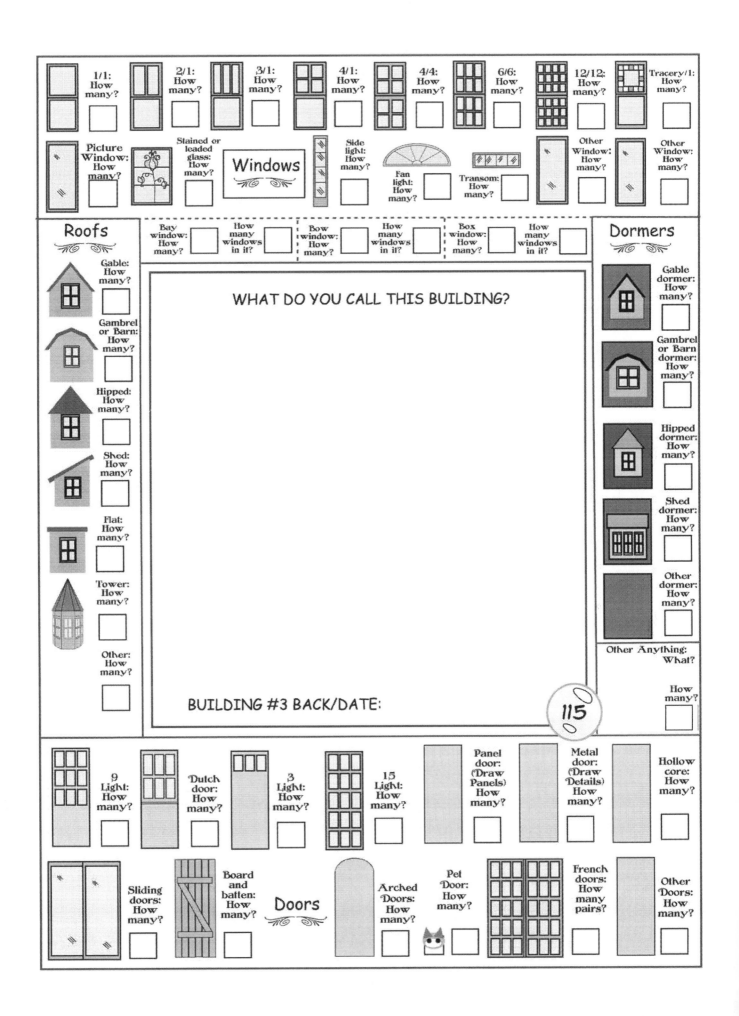

Windows

1/1: How many?
2/1: How many?
3/1: How many?
4/1: How many?
4/4: How many?
6/6: How many?
12/12: How many?
Tracery/1: How many?

Picture Window: How many?
Stained or leaded glass: How many?
Side light: How many?
Fan light: How many?
Transom: How many?
Other Window: How many?
Other Window: How many?

Roofs

Bay window: How many?
How many windows in it?
Bow window: How many?
How many windows in it?
Box window: How many?
How many windows in it?

Dormers

Gable: How many?
Gambrel or Barn: How many?
Hipped: How many?
Shed: How many?
Flat: How many?
Tower: How many?
Other: How many?

WHAT DO YOU CALL THIS BUILDING?

BUILDING #3 BACK/DATE:

Gable dormer: How many?
Gambrel or Barn dormer: How many?
Hipped dormer: How many?
Shed dormer: How many?
Other dormer: How many?

Other Anything: What?
How many?

115

9 Light: How many?
Dutch door: How many?
3 Light: How many?
15 Light: How many?
Panel door: (Draw Panels) How many?
Metal door: (Draw Details) How many?
Hollow core: How many?

Sliding doors: How many?
Board and batten: How many?
Doors
Arched Doors: How many?
Pet Door: How many?
French doors: How many pairs?
Other Doors: How many?

UNUSUAL DOORS: DRAW THEM   UNUSUAL WINDOWS: DRAW THEM

BUILDING #3: RIGHT SIDE

ROOF:

WHAT IS YOUR ROOF MADE OF?

_____

WHAT STICKS OUT OF YOUR ROOF:

CHIMNEYS?

YES ☐   NO ☐

HOW MANY CHIMNEYS? ☐

WHAT ARE THE CHIMNEYS MADE OF?

_____

_____

VENT STACK OR ELECTRIC LINES?

YES, ☐   NO ☐   (THESE
                  LOOK LIKE
                  PIPES.)

FOUNDATION:

WHAT KIND OF FOUNDATION
DOES YOUR HOUSE HAVE?

_____

WHAT STICKS OUT OF YOUR
FOUNDATION?

_____

_____

_____

_____

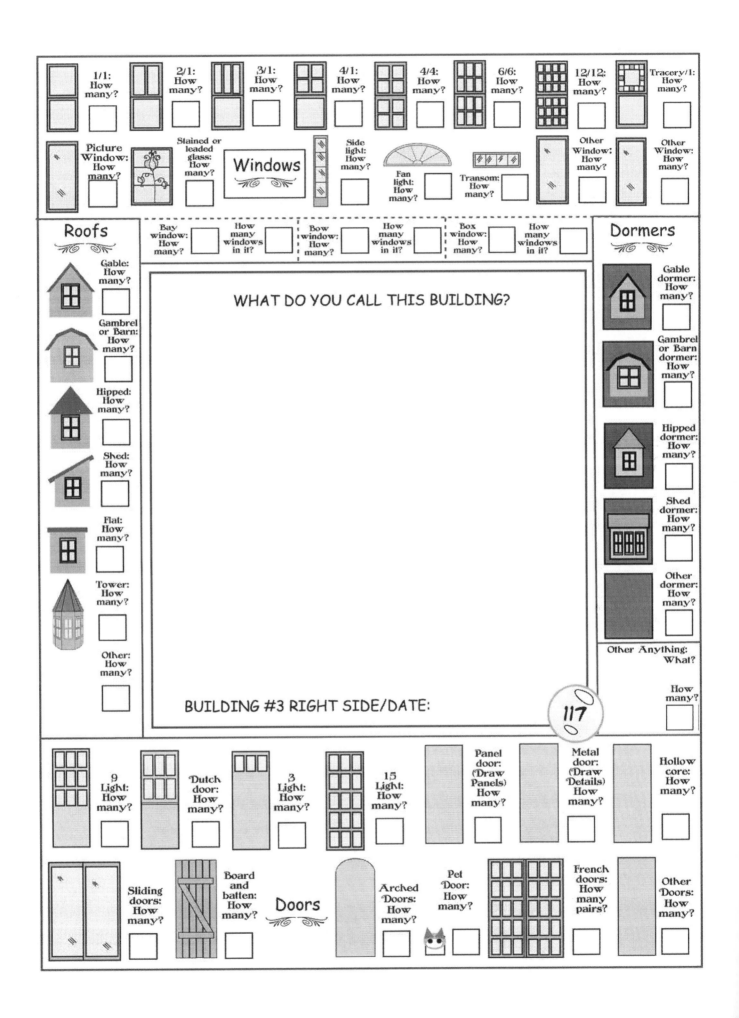

Windows

1/1: How many? ☐
2/1: How many? ☐
3/1: How many? ☐
4/1: How many? ☐
4/4: How many? ☐
6/6: How many? ☐
12/12: How many? ☐
Tracery/1: How many? ☐

Picture Window: How many? ☐
Stained or leaded glass: How many? ☐
Side light: How many? ☐
Fan light: How many? ☐
Transom: How many? ☐
Other Window: How many? ☐
Other Window: How many? ☐

Bay window: How many? ☐ How many windows in it? ☐
Bow window: How many? ☐ How many windows in it? ☐
Box window: How many? ☐ How many windows in it? ☐

Roofs

Gable: How many? ☐
Gambrel or Barn: How many? ☐
Hipped: How many? ☐
Shed: How many? ☐
Flat: How many? ☐
Tower: How many? ☐
Other: How many? ☐

WHAT DO YOU CALL THIS BUILDING?

BUILDING #3 RIGHT SIDE/DATE:

Dormers

Gable dormer: How many? ☐
Gambrel or Barn dormer: How many? ☐
Hipped dormer: How many? ☐
Shed dormer: How many? ☐
Other dormer: How many? ☐

Other Anything: What?

How many? ☐

117

Doors

9 Light: How many? ☐
Dutch door: How many? ☐
3 Light: How many? ☐
15 Light: How many? ☐
Panel door: (Draw Panels) How many? ☐
Metal door: (Draw Details) How many? ☐
Hollow core: How many? ☐

Sliding doors: How many? ☐
Board and batten: How many? ☐
Arched Doors: How many? ☐
Pet Door: How many? ☐
French doors: How many pairs? ☐
Other Doors: How many? ☐

FLOOR PLAN BASEMENT

WHICH
WAY IS
NORTH?

BUILDING #3

NAME OF BUILDING:

DATE:

How many rooms? ☐

Name the rooms and note what the ceiling, floor, and walls are made of.

#	NAME OF ROOM	CEILING	WALLS	FLOOR
1				
2				
3				
4				
5				
6				
7				
8				

FLOOR PLAN FIRST FLOOR

WHICH
WAY IS
NORTH?

BUILDING #3

NAME OF BUILDING:

How many rooms? ☐

DATE:

Name the rooms and note what the ceiling, floor, and walls are made of.

#	NAME OF ROOM	CEILING	WALLS	FLOOR
1				
2				
3				
4				
5				
6				
7				
8				

FLOOR PLAN SECOND FLOOR

BUILDING #3

NAME OF BUILDING:

DATE:

How many rooms?

Name the rooms and note what the ceiling, floor, and walls are made of.

#	NAME OF ROOM	CEILING	WALLS	FLOOR
1				
2				
3				
4				
5				
6				
7				
8				

FLOOR PLAN THIRD FLOOR

BUILDING #3

NAME OF BUILDING:

DATE:

How many rooms? ☐

Name the rooms and note what the ceiling, floor, and walls are made of.

#	NAME OF ROOM	CEILING	WALLS	FLOOR
1				
2				
3				
4				
5				
6				
7				
8				

FLOOR PLAN FOURTH FLOOR

WHICH
WAY IS
NORTH?

BUILDING #3

NAME OF BUILDING:

How many rooms? ☐

DATE:

Name the rooms and note what the ceiling, floor, and walls are made of.

#	NAME OF ROOM	CEILING	WALLS	FLOOR
1				
2				
3				
4				
5				
6				
7				
8				

FLOOR PLAN ATTIC

N

WHICH
WAY IS
NORTH?

BUILDING #3

NAME OF BUILDING:

How many rooms? ☐

DATE:

Name the rooms and note what the ceiling, floor, and walls are made of.

#	NAME OF ROOM	CEILING	WALLS	FLOOR
1				
2				
3				
4				
5				
6				
7				
8				

123

PLOT PLAN BUILDING #3
NAME OF BUILDING:

WHICH
WAY IS
NORTH?

DATE:

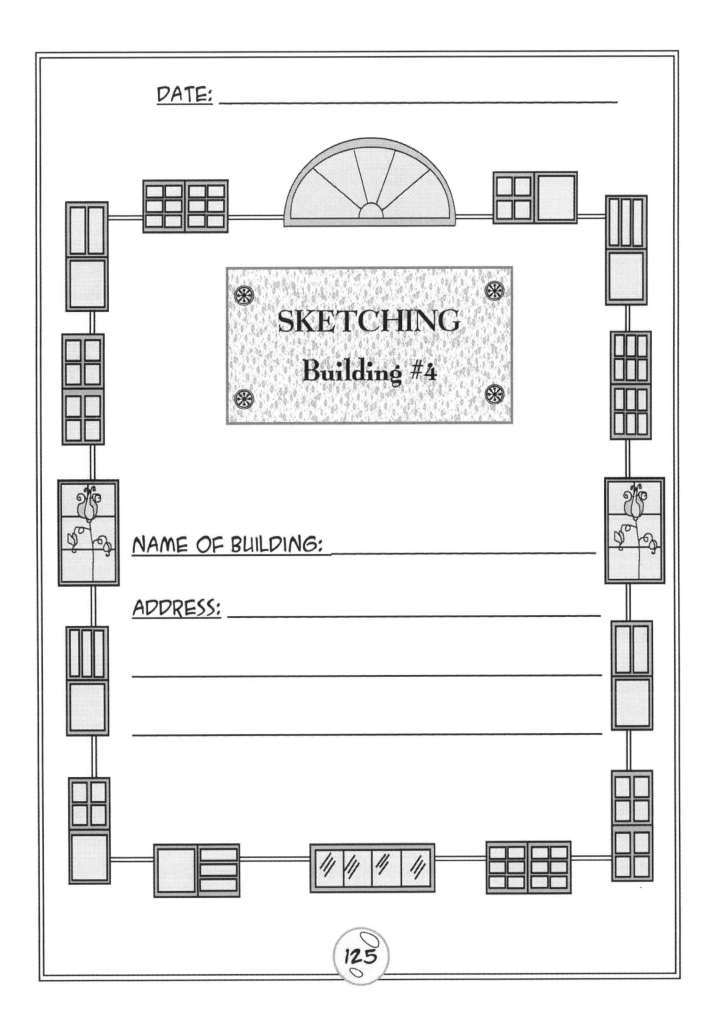

DATE: _____

SKETCHING
Building #4

NAME OF BUILDING: _____

ADDRESS: _____

_____

_____

125

UNUSUAL DOORS: DRAW THEM   UNUSUAL WINDOWS: DRAW THEM

BUILDING #4: FRONT

ROOF: FOUNDATION:

WHAT IS YOUR ROOF MADE OF?   WHAT KIND OF FOUNDATION
                                   DOES YOUR HOUSE HAVE?
_____

WHAT STICKS OUT OF YOUR ROOF:

CHIMNEYS?   _____

YES ☐   NO ☐   WHAT STICKS OUT OF YOUR
                                   FOUNDATION?
HOW MANY CHIMNEYS? ☐

WHAT ARE THE CHIMNEYS MADE OF?   _____

_____   _____

_____   _____

VENT STACK OR ELECTRIC LINES?   _____

YES. ☐   NO ☐ (THESE
               LOOK LIKE
               PIPES.)

126

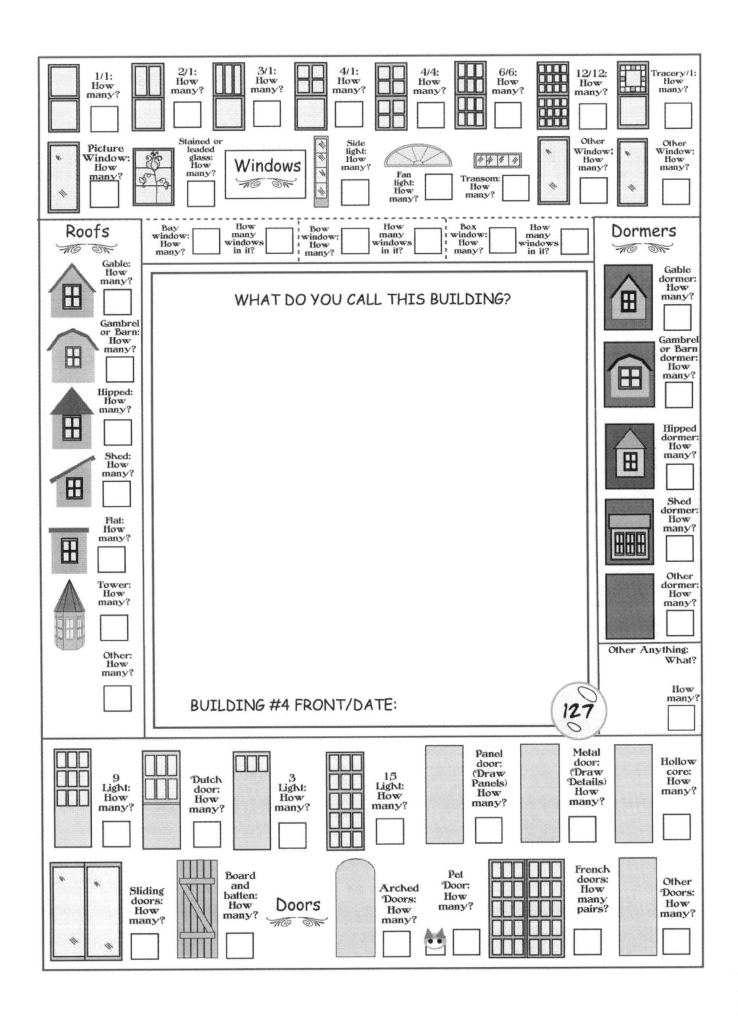

Windows

1/1: How many? ☐

2/1: How many? ☐

3/1: How many? ☐

4/1: How many? ☐

4/4: How many? ☐

6/6: How many? ☐

12/12: How many? ☐

Tracery/1: How many? ☐

Picture Window: How many? ☐

Stained or leaded glass: How many? ☐

Side light: How many? ☐

Fan light: How many? ☐

Transom: How many? ☐

Other Window: How many? ☐

Other Window: How many? ☐

Bay window: How many? ☐ How many windows in it? ☐

Bow window: How many? ☐ How many windows in it? ☐

Box window: How many? ☐ How many windows in it? ☐

Roofs

Gable: How many? ☐

Gambrel or Barn: How many? ☐

Hipped: How many? ☐

Shed: How many? ☐

Flat: How many? ☐

Tower: How many? ☐

Other: How many? ☐

Dormers

Gable dormer: How many? ☐

Gambrel or Barn dormer: How many? ☐

Hipped dormer: How many? ☐

Shed dormer: How many? ☐

Other dormer: How many? ☐

Other Anything: What?

How many? ☐

WHAT DO YOU CALL THIS BUILDING?

BUILDING #4 FRONT/DATE:

127

Doors

9 Light: How many? ☐

Dutch door: How many? ☐

3 Light: How many? ☐

15 Light: How many? ☐

Panel door: (Draw Panels) How many? ☐

Metal door: (Draw Details) How many? ☐

Hollow core: How many? ☐

Sliding doors: How many? ☐

Board and batten: How many? ☐

Arched Doors: How many? ☐

Pet Door: How many? ☐

French doors: How many pairs? ☐

Other Doors: How many? ☐

UNUSUAL DOORS: DRAW THEM   UNUSUAL WINDOWS: DRAW THEM

BUILDING #4: LEFT SIDE

ROOF: FOUNDATION:

WHAT IS YOUR ROOF MADE OF?   WHAT KIND OF FOUNDATION
                                         DOES YOUR HOUSE HAVE?
_____

WHAT STICKS OUT OF YOUR ROOF:

CHIMNEYS?   _____

YES ☐   NO ☐   WHAT STICKS OUT OF YOUR
                                         FOUNDATION?
HOW MANY CHIMNEYS? ☐
                                         _____
WHAT ARE THE CHIMNEYS MADE OF?

_____   _____

_____   _____

VENT STACK OR ELECTRIC LINES?   _____

YES, ☐   NO ☐   (THESE
                 LOOK LIKE
                 PIPES.)

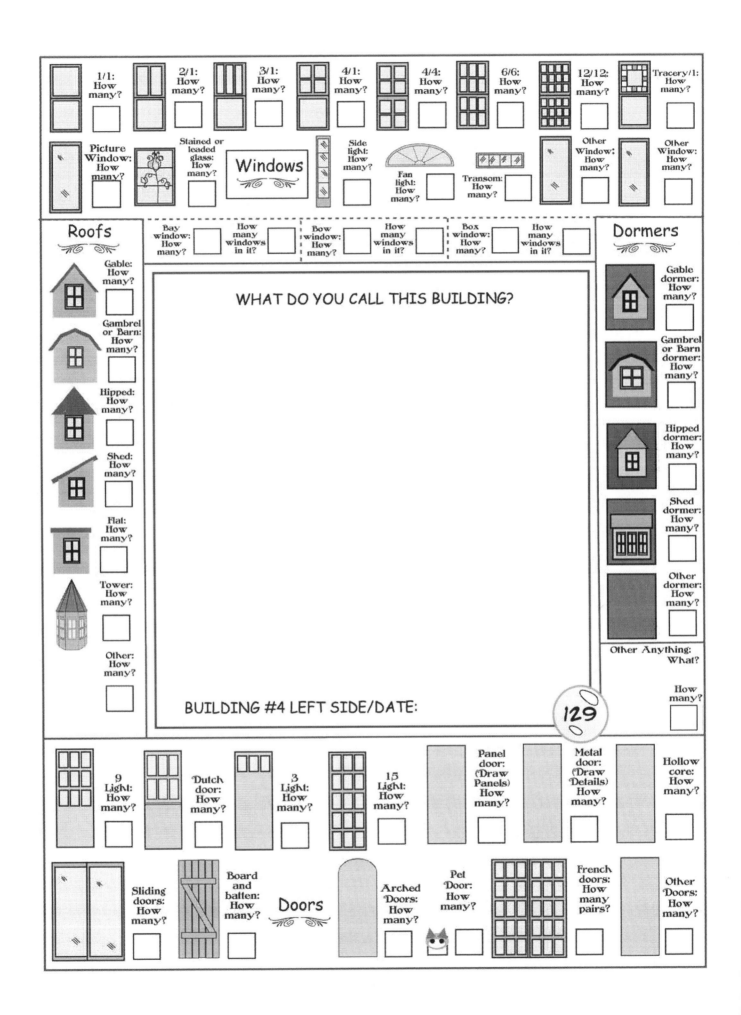

Windows

1/1: How many?

2/1: How many?

3/1: How many?

4/1: How many?

4/4: How many?

6/6: How many?

12/12: How many?

Tracery/1: How many?

Picture Window: How many?

Stained or leaded glass: How many?

Side light: How many?

Fan light: How many?

Transom: How many?

Other Window: How many?

Other Window: How many?

Bay window: How many?

How many windows in it?

Bow window: How many?

How many windows in it?

Box window: How many?

How many windows in it?

Roofs

Gable: How many?

Gambrel or Barn: How many?

Hipped: How many?

Shed: How many?

Flat: How many?

Tower: How many?

Other: How many?

WHAT DO YOU CALL THIS BUILDING?

BUILDING #4 LEFT SIDE/DATE:

129

Dormers

Gable dormer: How many?

Gambrel or Barn dormer: How many?

Hipped dormer: How many?

Shed dormer: How many?

Other dormer: How many?

Other Anything: What?

How many?

Doors

9 Light: How many?

Dutch door: How many?

3 Light: How many?

15 Light: How many?

Panel door: (Draw Panels) How many?

Metal door: (Draw Details) How many?

Hollow core: How many?

Sliding doors: How many?

Board and batten: How many?

Arched Doors: How many?

Pet Door: How many?

French doors: How many pairs?

Other Doors: How many?

UNUSUAL DOORS: DRAW THEM   UNUSUAL WINDOWS: DRAW THEM

BUILDING #4: BACK

ROOF: FOUNDATION:

WHAT IS YOUR ROOF MADE OF?   WHAT KIND OF FOUNDATION
                                         DOES YOUR HOUSE HAVE?
_____

WHAT STICKS OUT OF YOUR ROOF:

CHIMNEYS?   _____

YES ☐   NO ☐   WHAT STICKS OUT OF YOUR
                                         FOUNDATION?
HOW MANY CHIMNEYS? ☐

WHAT ARE THE CHIMNEYS MADE OF?   _____

_____   _____

_____   _____

VENT STACK OR ELECTRIC LINES?   _____

YES. ☐   NO ☐   (THESE   _____
                LOOK LIKE
                PIPES.)

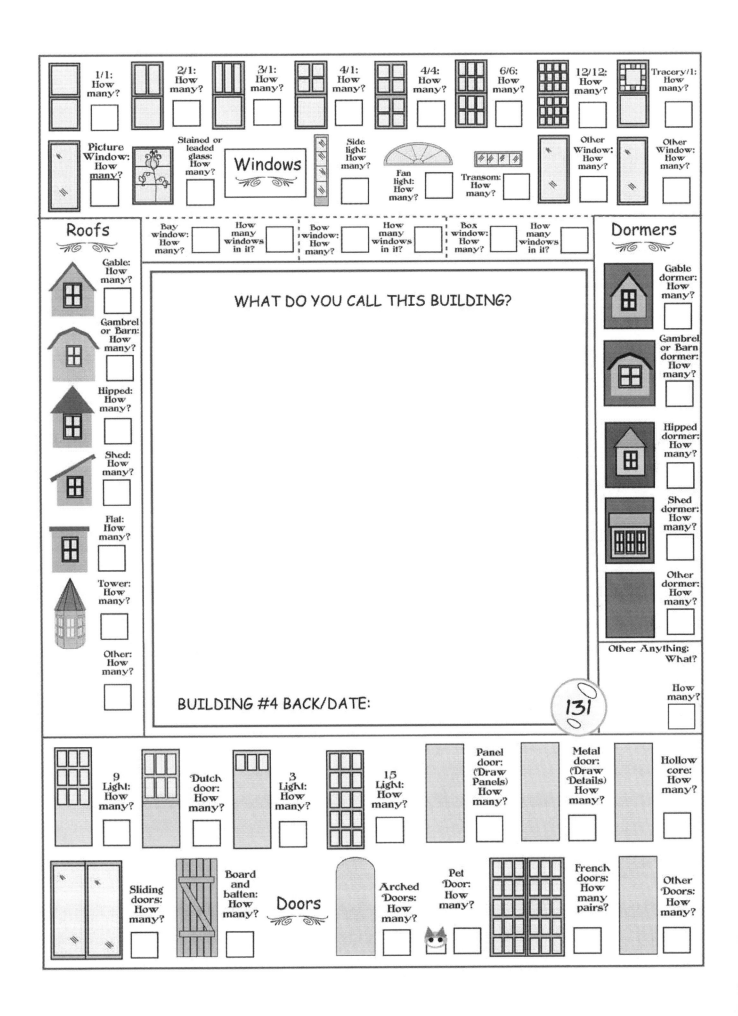

Windows

1/1: How many? ☐
2/1: How many? ☐
3/1: How many? ☐
4/1: How many? ☐
4/4: How many? ☐
6/6: How many? ☐
12/12: How many? ☐
Tracery/1: How many? ☐

Picture Window: How many? ☐
Stained or leaded glass: How many? ☐
Side light: How many? ☐
Fan light: How many? ☐
Transom: How many? ☐
Other Window: How many? ☐
Other Window: How many? ☐

Bay window: How many? ☐
How many windows in it? ☐
Bow window: How many? ☐
How many windows in it? ☐
Box window: How many? ☐
How many windows in it? ☐

Roofs

Gable: How many? ☐
Gambrel or Barn: How many? ☐
Hipped: How many? ☐
Shed: How many? ☐
Flat: How many? ☐
Tower: How many? ☐
Other: How many? ☐

WHAT DO YOU CALL THIS BUILDING?

BUILDING #4 BACK/DATE:

131

Dormers

Gable dormer: How many? ☐
Gambrel or Barn dormer: How many? ☐
Hipped dormer: How many? ☐
Shed dormer: How many? ☐
Other dormer: How many? ☐

Other Anything: What?
How many? ☐

Doors

9 Light: How many? ☐
Dutch door: How many? ☐
3 Light: How many? ☐
15 Light: How many? ☐
Panel door: (Draw Panels) How many? ☐
Metal door: (Draw Details) How many? ☐
Hollow core: How many? ☐

Sliding doors: How many? ☐
Board and batten: How many? ☐
Arched Doors: How many? ☐
Pet Door: How many? ☐
French doors: How many pairs? ☐
Other Doors: How many? ☐

UNUSUAL DOORS: DRAW THEM   UNUSUAL WINDOWS: DRAW THEM

BUILDING #4: RIGHT SIDE

ROOF:

WHAT IS YOUR ROOF MADE OF?

_____

WHAT STICKS OUT OF YOUR ROOF:

CHIMNEYS?

YES ☐   NO ☐

HOW MANY CHIMNEYS? ☐

WHAT ARE THE CHIMNEYS MADE OF?

_____

_____

VENT STACK OR ELECTRIC LINES?

YES. ☐   NO ☐   (THESE
LOOK LIKE
PIPES.)

FOUNDATION:

WHAT KIND OF FOUNDATION
DOES YOUR HOUSE HAVE?

_____

WHAT STICKS OUT OF YOUR
FOUNDATION?

_____

_____

_____

_____

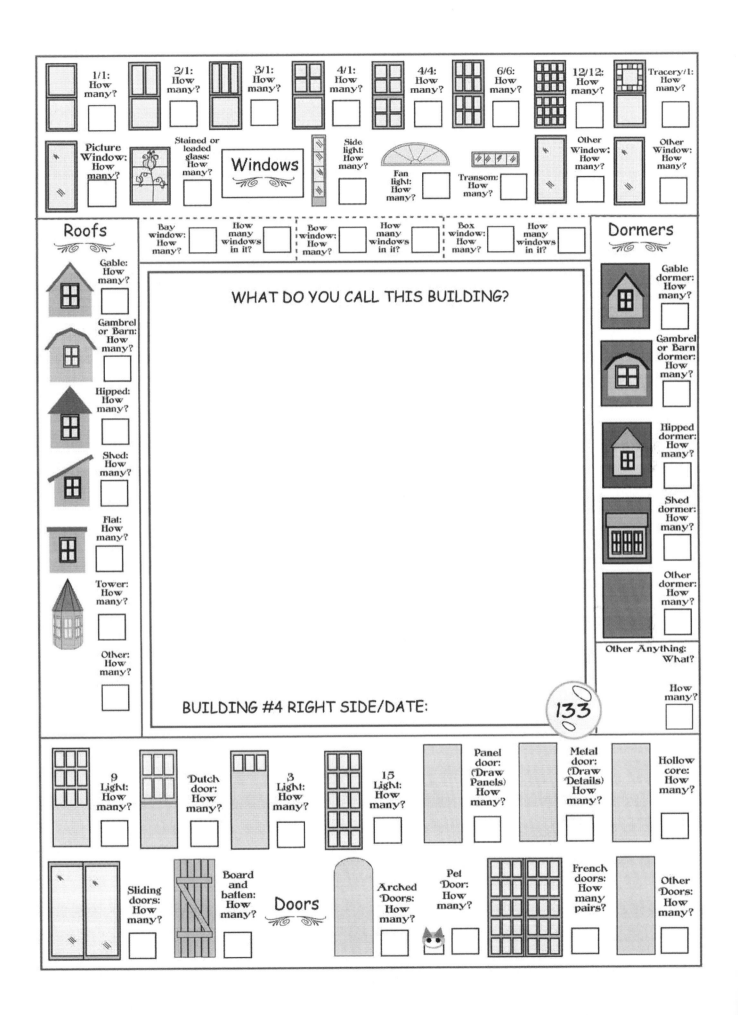

Windows

1/1: How many? ☐
2/1: How many? ☐
3/1: How many? ☐
4/1: How many? ☐
4/4: How many? ☐
6/6: How many? ☐
12/12: How many? ☐
Tracery/1: How many? ☐

Picture Window: How many? ☐
Stained or leaded glass: How many? ☐
Side light: How many? ☐
Fan light: How many? ☐
Transom: How many? ☐
Other Window: How many? ☐
Other Window: How many? ☐

Bay window: How many? ☐ How many windows in it? ☐
Bow window: How many? ☐ How many windows in it? ☐
Box window: How many? ☐ How many windows in it? ☐

Roofs

Gable: How many? ☐
Gambrel or Barn: How many? ☐
Hipped: How many? ☐
Shed: How many? ☐
Flat: How many? ☐
Tower: How many? ☐
Other: How many? ☐

WHAT DO YOU CALL THIS BUILDING?

BUILDING #4 RIGHT SIDE/DATE:

133

Dormers

Gable dormer: How many? ☐
Gambrel or Barn dormer: How many? ☐
Hipped dormer: How many? ☐
Shed dormer: How many? ☐
Other dormer: How many? ☐

Other Anything: What?
How many? ☐

Doors

9 Light: How many? ☐
Dutch door: How many? ☐
3 Light: How many? ☐
15 Light: How many? ☐
Panel door: (Draw Panels) How many? ☐
Metal door: (Draw Details) How many? ☐
Hollow core: How many? ☐

Sliding doors: How many? ☐
Board and batten: How many? ☐
Arched Doors: How many? ☐
Pet Door: How many? ☐
French doors: How many pairs? ☐
Other Doors: How many? ☐

FLOOR PLAN BASEMENT

WHICH
WAY IS
NORTH?

BUILDING #4

NAME OF BUILDING:

DATE:

How many rooms?

Name the rooms and note what the ceiling, floor, and walls are made of.

#	NAME OF ROOM	CEILING	WALLS	FLOOR
1				
2				
3				
4				
5				
6				
7				
8				

134

FLOOR PLAN FIRST FLOOR

WHICH
WAY IS
NORTH?

BUILDING #4

NAME OF BUILDING:

DATE:

How many rooms? ☐

Name the rooms and note what the ceiling, floor, and walls are made of.

#	NAME OF ROOM	CEILING	WALLS	FLOOR
1				
2				
3				
4				
5				
6				
7				
8				

135

FLOOR PLAN SECOND FLOOR

WHICH
WAY IS
NORTH?

BUILDING #4

NAME OF BUILDING:

How many rooms? ☐

DATE:

Name the rooms and note what the ceiling, floor, and walls are made of.

#	NAME OF ROOM	CEILING	WALLS	FLOOR
1				
2				
3				
4				
5				
6				
7				
8				

FLOOR PLAN THIRD FLOOR

BUILDING #4

NAME OF BUILDING:

DATE:

How many rooms? ☐

Name the rooms and note what the ceiling, floor, and walls are made of.

#	NAME OF ROOM	CEILING	WALLS	FLOOR
1				
2				
3				
4				
5				
6				
7				
8				

137

FLOOR PLAN FOURTH FLOOR

BUILDING #4

NAME OF BUILDING:

How many rooms? ☐

DATE:

Name the rooms and note what the ceiling, floor, and walls are made of.

#	NAME OF ROOM	CEILING	WALLS	FLOOR
1				
2				
3				
4				
5				
6				
7				
8				

FLOOR PLAN ATTIC

WHICH
WAY IS
NORTH?

BUILDING #4

NAME OF BUILDING:

DATE:

How many rooms?

Name the rooms and note what the ceiling, floor, and walls are made of.

#	NAME OF ROOM	CEILING	WALLS	FLOOR
1				
2				
3				
4				
5				
6				
7				
8				

PLOT PLAN BUILDING #4
NAME OF BUILDING:

WHICH
WAY IS
NORTH?

DATE:

DATE: _____

SKETCHING
Building #5

NAME OF BUILDING: _____

ADDRESS: _____

_____

_____

UNUSUAL DOORS: DRAW THEM   UNUSUAL WINDOWS: DRAW THEM

BUILDING #5: FRONT

ROOF: FOUNDATION:

WHAT IS YOUR ROOF MADE OF?   WHAT KIND OF FOUNDATION
                                         DOES YOUR HOUSE HAVE?
_____

WHAT STICKS OUT OF YOUR ROOF:

CHIMNEYS?   _____

YES ☐   NO ☐   WHAT STICKS OUT OF YOUR
                                         FOUNDATION?
HOW MANY CHIMNEYS? ☐

                                         _____
WHAT ARE THE CHIMNEYS MADE OF?

                                         _____
_____

                                         _____
_____

                                         _____
VENT STACK OR ELECTRIC LINES?

                                         _____
YES. ☐   NO ☐   (THESE
                 LOOK LIKE
                 PIPES.)

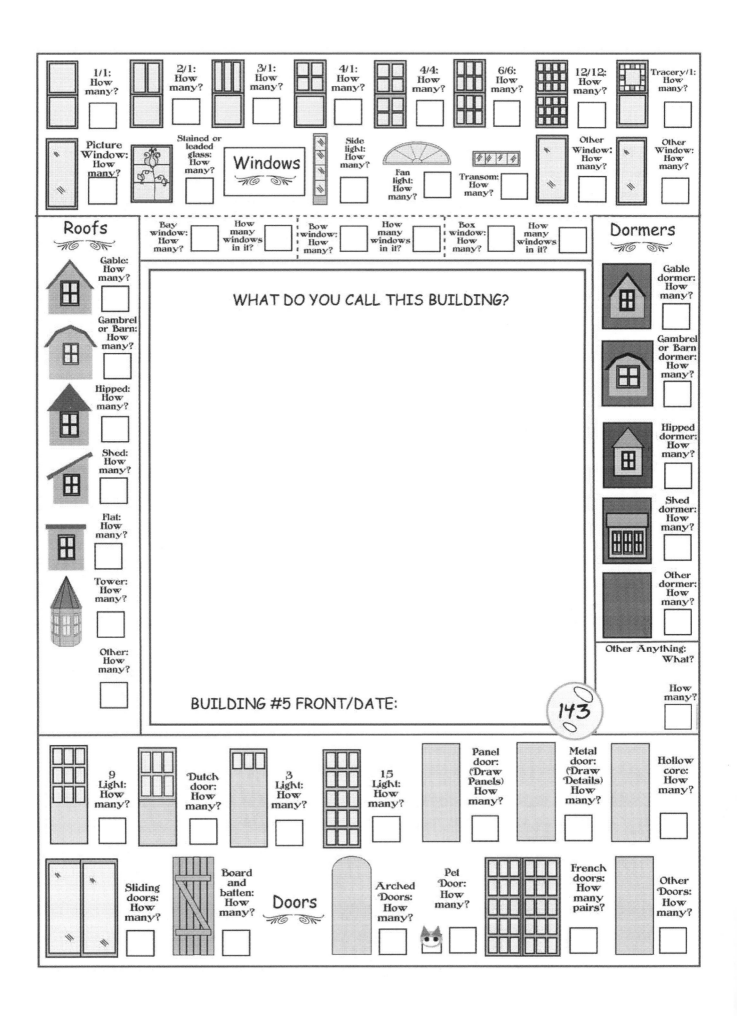

Windows (top row):

1/1: How many?
2/1: How many?
3/1: How many?
4/1: How many?
4/4: How many?
6/6: How many?
12/12: How many?
Tracery/1: How many?

Windows (second row):

Picture Window: How many?
Stained or leaded glass: How many?
Windows
Side light: How many?
Fan light: How many?
Transom: How many?
Other Window: How many?
Other Window: How many?

Bay window: How many?
How many windows in it?
Bow window: How many?
How many windows in it?
Box window: How many?
How many windows in it?

Roofs

Gable: How many?
Gambrel or Barn: How many?
Hipped: How many?
Shed: How many?
Flat: How many?
Tower: How many?
Other: How many?

Dormers

Gable dormer: How many?
Gambrel or Barn dormer: How many?
Hipped dormer: How many?
Shed dormer: How many?
Other dormer: How many?

Other Anything: What?
How many?

WHAT DO YOU CALL THIS BUILDING?

BUILDING #5 FRONT/DATE:

143

Doors

9 Light: How many?
Dutch door: How many?
3 Light: How many?
15 Light: How many?
Panel door: (Draw Panels) How many?
Metal door: (Draw Details) How many?
Hollow core: How many?

Sliding doors: How many?
Board and batten: How many?
Doors
Arched Doors: How many?
Pet Door: How many?
French doors: How many pairs?
Other Doors: How many?

UNUSUAL DOORS: DRAW THEM   UNUSUAL WINDOWS: DRAW THEM

BUILDING #5: LEFT SIDE

ROOF: FOUNDATION:

WHAT IS YOUR ROOF MADE OF?   WHAT KIND OF FOUNDATION
                                        DOES YOUR HOUSE HAVE?
_____

WHAT STICKS OUT OF YOUR ROOF:

CHIMNEYS?   _____

YES ☐   NO ☐

                                        WHAT STICKS OUT OF YOUR
HOW MANY CHIMNEYS? ☐   FOUNDATION?

WHAT ARE THE CHIMNEYS MADE OF?   _____

_____   _____

_____   _____

VENT STACK OR ELECTRIC LINES?   _____

YES. ☐   NO ☐   (THESE
                 LOOK LIKE
                 PIPES.)

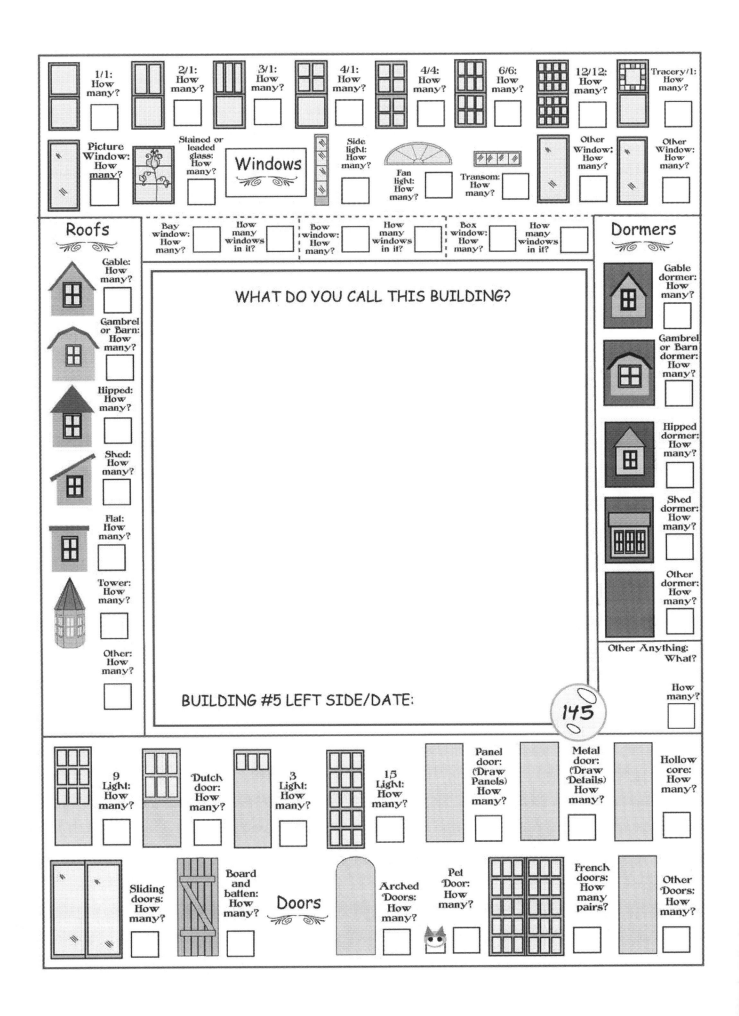

Windows

1/1: How many? ☐
2/1: How many? ☐
3/1: How many? ☐
4/1: How many? ☐
4/4: How many? ☐
6/6: How many? ☐
12/12: How many? ☐
Tracery/1: How many? ☐

Picture Window: How many? ☐
Stained or leaded glass: How many? ☐
Side light: How many? ☐
Fan light: How many? ☐
Transom: How many? ☐
Other Window: How many? ☐
Other Window: How many? ☐

Bay window: How many? ☐ How many windows in it? ☐
Bow window: How many? ☐ How many windows in it? ☐
Box window: How many? ☐ How many windows in it? ☐

Roofs

Gable: How many? ☐
Gambrel or Barn: How many? ☐
Hipped: How many? ☐
Shed: How many? ☐
Flat: How many? ☐
Tower: How many? ☐
Other: How many? ☐

WHAT DO YOU CALL THIS BUILDING?

BUILDING #5 LEFT SIDE/DATE:

Dormers

Gable dormer: How many? ☐
Gambrel or Barn dormer: How many? ☐
Hipped dormer: How many? ☐
Shed dormer: How many? ☐
Other dormer: How many? ☐

Other Anything: What?

How many? ☐

145

Doors

9 Light: How many? ☐
Dutch door: How many? ☐
3 Light: How many? ☐
15 Light: How many? ☐
Panel door: (Draw Panels) How many? ☐
Metal door: (Draw Details) How many? ☐
Hollow core: How many? ☐

Sliding doors: How many? ☐
Board and batten: How many? ☐
Arched Doors: How many? ☐
Pet Door: How many? ☐
French doors: How many pairs? ☐
Other Doors: How many? ☐

UNUSUAL DOORS: DRAW THEM   UNUSUAL WINDOWS: DRAW THEM

BUILDING #5: BACK

ROOF: FOUNDATION:

WHAT IS YOUR ROOF MADE OF?   WHAT KIND OF FOUNDATION
                                    DOES YOUR HOUSE HAVE?
_____

WHAT STICKS OUT OF YOUR ROOF:
                                    _____
CHIMNEYS?

YES ☐   NO ☐   WHAT STICKS OUT OF YOUR
                                    FOUNDATION?
HOW MANY CHIMNEYS? ☐

WHAT ARE THE CHIMNEYS MADE OF?   _____

_____   _____

_____   _____

VENT STACK OR ELECTRIC LINES?   _____

YES, ☐   NO ☐   (THESE
                 LOOK LIKE
                 PIPES.)

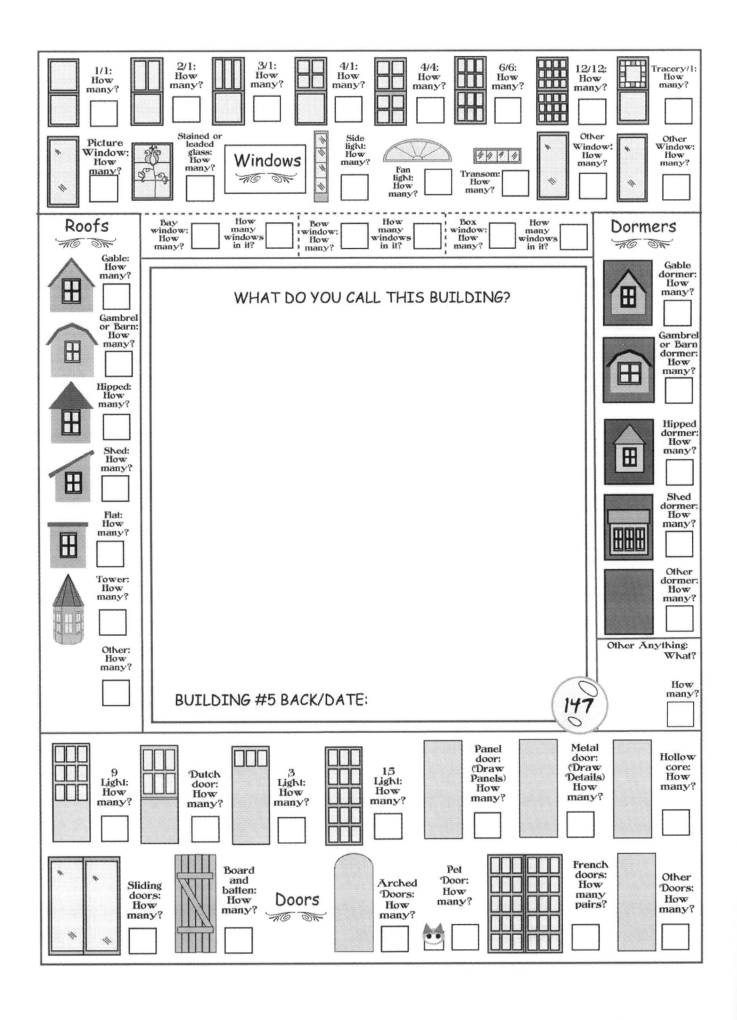

Windows

- 1/1: How many? ☐
- 2/1: How many? ☐
- 3/1: How many? ☐
- 4/1: How many? ☐
- 4/4: How many? ☐
- 6/6: How many? ☐
- 12/12: How many? ☐
- Tracery/1: How many? ☐
- Picture Window: How many? ☐
- Stained or leaded glass: How many? ☐
- Side light: How many? ☐
- Fan light: How many? ☐
- Transom: How many? ☐
- Other Window: How many? ☐
- Other Window: How many? ☐
- Bay window: How many? ☐ How many windows in it? ☐
- Bow window: How many? ☐ How many windows in it? ☐
- Box window: How many? ☐ How many windows in it? ☐

Roofs

- Gable: How many? ☐
- Gambrel or Barn: How many? ☐
- Hipped: How many? ☐
- Shed: How many? ☐
- Flat: How many? ☐
- Tower: How many? ☐
- Other: How many? ☐

Dormers

- Gable dormer: How many? ☐
- Gambrel or Barn dormer: How many? ☐
- Hipped dormer: How many? ☐
- Shed dormer: How many? ☐
- Other dormer: How many? ☐
- Other Anything: What? How many? ☐

WHAT DO YOU CALL THIS BUILDING?

BUILDING #5 BACK/DATE:

147

Doors

- 9 Light: How many? ☐
- Dutch door: How many? ☐
- 3 Light: How many? ☐
- 15 Light: How many? ☐
- Panel door: (Draw Panels) How many? ☐
- Metal door: (Draw Details) How many? ☐
- Hollow core: How many? ☐
- Sliding doors: How many? ☐
- Board and batten: How many? ☐
- Arched Doors: How many? ☐
- Pet Door: How many? ☐
- French doors: How many pairs? ☐
- Other Doors: How many? ☐

UNUSUAL DOORS: DRAW THEM   UNUSUAL WINDOWS: DRAW THEM

BUILDING #5: RIGHT SIDE

ROOF: FOUNDATION:

WHAT IS YOUR ROOF MADE OF?   WHAT KIND OF FOUNDATION
                                           DOES YOUR HOUSE HAVE?
_____

WHAT STICKS OUT OF YOUR ROOF:

CHIMNEYS?   _____

YES ☐   NO ☐
                                           WHAT STICKS OUT OF YOUR
HOW MANY CHIMNEYS? ☐   FOUNDATION?

WHAT ARE THE CHIMNEYS MADE OF?
                                           _____
_____
                                           _____

_____
                                           _____

VENT STACK OR ELECTRIC LINES?
                                           _____
YES. ☐   NO ☐   (THESE
                   LOOK LIKE
                   PIPES.)

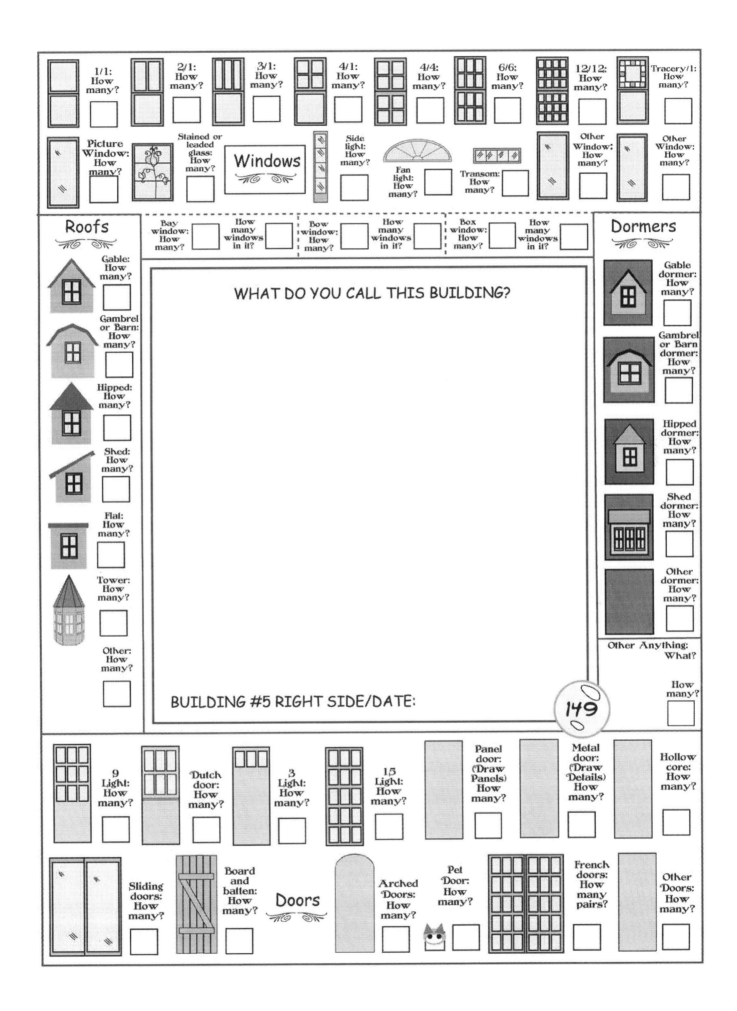

Windows

1/1: How many?

2/1: How many?

3/1: How many?

4/1: How many?

4/4: How many?

6/6: How many?

12/12: How many?

Tracery/1: How many?

Picture Window: How many?

Stained or leaded glass: How many?

Side light: How many?

Fan light: How many?

Transom: How many?

Other Window: How many?

Other Window: How many?

Bay window: How many? How many windows in it?

Bow window: How many? How many windows in it?

Box window: How many? How many windows in it?

Roofs

Gable: How many?

Gambrel or Barn: How many?

Hipped: How many?

Shed: How many?

Flat: How many?

Tower: How many?

Other: How many?

Dormers

Gable dormer: How many?

Gambrel or Barn dormer: How many?

Hipped dormer: How many?

Shed dormer: How many?

Other dormer: How many?

Other Anything: What?

How many?

WHAT DO YOU CALL THIS BUILDING?

BUILDING #5 RIGHT SIDE/DATE:

149

Doors

9 Light: How many?

Dutch door: How many?

3 Light: How many?

15 Light: How many?

Panel door: (Draw Panels) How many?

Metal door: (Draw Details) How many?

Hollow core: How many?

Sliding doors: How many?

Board and batten: How many?

Arched Doors: How many?

Pet Door: How many?

French doors: How many pairs?

Other Doors: How many?

FLOOR PLAN BASEMENT

WHICH
WAY IS
NORTH?

BUILDING #5

NAME OF BUILDING:

DATE:

How many rooms?

Name the rooms and note what the ceiling, floor, and walls are made of.

#	NAME OF ROOM	CEILING	WALLS	FLOOR
1				
2				
3				
4				
5				
6				
7				
8				

FLOOR PLAN FIRST FLOOR

BUILDING #5

NAME OF BUILDING:

How many rooms? ☐

DATE:

Name the rooms and note what the ceiling, floor, and walls are made of.

#	NAME OF ROOM	CEILING	WALLS	FLOOR
1				
2				
3				
4				
5				
6				
7				
8				

FLOOR PLAN SECOND FLOOR

WHICH
WAY IS
NORTH?

BUILDING #5

NAME OF BUILDING:

How many rooms? ☐

DATE:

Name the rooms and note what the ceiling, floor, and walls are made of.

#	NAME OF ROOM	CEILING	WALLS	FLOOR
1				
2				
3				
4				
5				
6				
7				
8				

FLOOR PLAN THIRD FLOOR

WHICH
WAY IS
NORTH?

BUILDING #5

NAME OF BUILDING:

How many rooms? ☐

DATE:

Name the rooms and note what the ceiling, floor, and walls are made of.

#	NAME OF ROOM	CEILING	WALLS	FLOOR
1				
2				
3				
4				
5				
6				
7				
8				

FLOOR PLAN FOURTH FLOOR

WHICH
WAY IS
NORTH?

BUILDING #5

NAME OF BUILDING:

How many rooms? ☐

DATE:

Name the rooms and note what the ceiling, floor, and walls are made of.

#	NAME OF ROOM	CEILING	WALLS	FLOOR
1				
2				
3				
4				
5				
6				
7				
8				

FLOOR PLAN ATTIC

BUILDING #5

NAME OF BUILDING:

DATE:

How many rooms?

Name the rooms and note what the ceiling, floor, and walls are made of.

#	NAME OF ROOM	CEILING	WALLS	FLOOR
1				
2				
3				
4				
5				
6				
7				
8				

PLOT PLAN BUILDING #5
NAME OF BUILDING:

WHICH
WAY IS
NORTH?

 DATE:

IMAGINING WONDERFUL CHANGES
THE DAY DREAMER'S PAGES

IT IS INTERESTING TO NOTE WHAT THE ROOMS
IN YOUR HOUSE HAVE IN COMMON AND
WHETHER, OR NOT, IT SUITS YOUR FAMILY.
WHAT IS TERRIFIC ABOUT YOUR HOUSE?

Old trunks
Books
Movies
Toys
Stuffed animals

Tower
Secret Room
Fort
Indoor pond
Balcony

WHAT IS THERE ABOUT YOUR HOUSE THAT DOESN'T WORK FOR YOUR FAMILY?

Old trunks
Books
Movies
Toys
Stuffed animals

Tower
Secret Room
Fort
Indoor pond
Balcony

WHAT DO YOU WISH
YOUR HOUSE HAD
BUT IT DOESN'T?

_____

_____

_____

_____

_____

_____

_____

_____

_____

_____

_____

_____

Old trunks
Books
Movies
Toys
Stuffed animals

Tower
Secret Room
Fort
Indoor pond
Balcony

WHAT HAVE YOU SEEN IN OTHER PEOPLES' HOUSES THAT <u>WOULD</u> WORK IN YOURS?

Old trunks
Books
Movies
Toys
Stuffed animals

Tower
Secret Room
Fort
Indoor pond
Balcony

WHAT HAVE YOU SEEN IN OTHER PEOPLES' HOUSES THAT YOU <u>WOULDN'T</u> WANT IN YOURS?

Old trunks
Books
Movies
Toys
Stuffed animals

Tower
Secret Room
Fort
Indoor pond
Balcony

Favorite Things

WHAT ARE YOUR FAVORITE THINGS ABOUT YOUR HOUSE?

_____

_____

_____

_____

_____

_____

_____

_____

_____

_____

_____

Barn
Guest house
Courtyard
Fountain
Transoms
French doors
Diamond-paned windows
Lie in Bed & look out windows

Pond
Boating
Raspberries
Fruit trees
Playhouse
Trees for climbing
Children nearby
Walk to town

Think of a
favorite place:

Fantasy Page #1

How could your
house be changed
to be like that?

_____

_____

_____

_____

_____

_____

_____

_____

_____

_____

_____

_____

_____

_____

_____

_____

In Rockland, Maine there is an ice cream parlor called the Klondike Creamery. At Christmas time I like to sit in one of the window seats with the jumble of the pillows they have there, at the teeny marble-topped tables, and just to look out at the street, amidst the garlands of balsam trimmings, and tiny white Christmas lights and to eat ice cream. How could I have that same magic at my house? I'll pick up some ice cream on the way home! Haha! No, seriously...

-Window seat
- Lots of pillows
-Marble-topped table
- Tiny Christmas Lights
- Garlands of Balsam
- Ice cream

164

Think of a
favorite place:

Fantasy Page
#2

How could your
house be changed
to be like that?

In Dade City, Florida an old car showroom
was remodeled into a restaurant called
Kokopelli's. It has interior windows and a white
stucco Kiva fireplace in the corner of the room
the warmth, and smell of the wood burning
the crackle of the flames and the sight
of the dancing fire is terrific. Oh, and the
food is delicious too.

- Antique
wood
windows
indoors
- Fireplace in
dining room

Think of a favorite place:

Fantasy Page #3

How could your house be changed to be like that?

1967, Nantucket, Grandparents' Farmhouse:
The formal front entry was rarely used. It was more of a museum with old bottles on the window ledge and colored glass balls in a net and an organ with ivory keys and knobs. The entry was filled with light and it sparkled through the bottles. On the wall was a leather strap with bells on it. There were giant shells and coins. Our ancestors were ship captains and ship owners so there were many things from their travels. My cousin, Lynn, and I would play in this room for hours surrounded by things from all over the world.

- Collection of interesting things
- Deep Window ledge
- Place where treasures lie undisturbed

Where Do You Go?
Twelve Weeks of Your
Annual Travels

Where do you go?

January

Choose seven days...

Monday Date:	
Tuesday Date:	
Wednesday Date:	
Thursday Date:	
Friday Date:	
Saturday Date:	
Sunday Date:	

Where do you go?  **February** **Choose seven days...**

Monday Date:	
Tuesday Date:	
Wednesday Date:	
Thursday Date:	
Friday Date:	
Saturday Date:	
Sunday Date:	

Where do you go?

March

Choose seven days...

Monday **Date:**	
Tuesday **Date:**	
Wednesday **Date:**	
Thursday **Date:**	
Friday **Date:**	
Saturday **Date:**	
Sunday **Date:**	

Where do you go?

April

Choose seven days...

Monday Date:	
Tuesday Date:	
Wednesday Date:	
Thursday Date:	
Friday Date:	
Saturday Date:	
Sunday Date:	

Where do you go?

May

Choose seven days...

Monday Date:	
Tuesday Date:	
Wednesday Date:	
Thursday Date:	
Friday Date:	
Saturday Date:	
Sunday Date:	

Where do you go?

June

Choose seven days...

Monday **Date:**	
Tuesday **Date:**	
Wednesday **Date:**	
Thursday **Date:**	
Friday **Date:**	
Saturday **Date:**	
Sunday **Date:**	

Where do
you go?

July

Choose
seven days...

Monday Date:	
Tuesday Date:	
Wednesday Date:	
Thursday Date:	
Friday Date:	
Saturday Date:	
Sunday Date:	

August

Monday **Date:**	
Tuesday **Date:**	
Wednesday **Date:**	
Thursday **Date:**	
Friday **Date:**	
Saturday **Date:**	
Sunday **Date:**	

Where do
you go?

September

Choose
seven days...

Monday Date:	
Tuesday Date:	
Wednesday Date:	
Thursday Date:	
Friday Date:	
Saturday Date:	
Sunday Date:	

Where do you go?

October

Choose seven days...

Monday Date:	
Tuesday Date:	
Wednesday Date:	
Thursday Date:	
Friday Date:	
Saturday Date:	
Sunday Date:	

177

Where do you go?

 November

Choose seven days...

Monday Date:	
Tuesday Date:	
Wednesday Date:	
Thursday Date:	
Friday Date:	
Saturday Date:	
Sunday Date:	

Where do you go?

December

Choose seven days...

Monday Date:	
Tuesday Date:	
Wednesday Date:	
Thursday Date:	
Friday Date:	
Saturday Date:	
Sunday Date:	

Windows

1/1: How many?

2/1: How many?

3/1: How many?

4/1: How many?

4/4: How many?

6/6: How many?

12/12: How many?

Tracer [...] Ho[...]

Picture Window: How many?

Stained or leaded glass: How many?

Side light: How many?

Fan [...]

Other Window How many?

[...] w:

Bay window: How many?

[...] wi[...]

How many windows in it?

Can't Draw? Doesn't Matter!

Roofs

Gable: How many?

Gambrel or Barn: How many?

Hipped: How many?

Shed: How many?

Flat: How many?

Tower: How many?

Other: How many?

[Dor]mers

Gable dormer: How many?

Gambrel or Barn dormer: How many?

Hipped dormer: How many?

Shed dormer: How many?

Other dormer: How many?

Other Anything: What?

How many?

DISCOVER THE SECRET LANGUAGE OF THE BUILDINGS AROUND YOU TODAY.

9 Light: How many?

Dutch door: How many?

3 Light: How many?

15 Light: How many?

Panel door: (Draw Panels) How many?

Metal door: (Draw Details) How many?

Hollow core: How many?

[B]oard and [b]atten: Doors How many?

Arched Doors: How many?

Pet Door: How many?

French doors: How many pairs?

Other Doors: How many?

Consider This...

WE NATURALLY WANT TO LOOK
THROUGH THE MIDDLE OF WINDOW
SPACES AND WINDOWS

A PERSON LOOKING THROUGH A WINDOW WISHES TO
BE IN THE CENTER OF THE WINDOW SPACE – THIS IS
THE MOST TRANQUIL PLACE TO BE AND TO
ENCOUNTER THERE A GLASS PANE, NOT A MUNTIN.
SO IT MAY BE BETTER TO PUT WINDOWS IN ODD
NUMBER ARRANGEMENTS – EITHER SINGLE
OR THREE OR FIVE.
ADDITIONALLY WHEN CHOOSING THE NUMBER OF
SMALL PANES IT MAY BE MORE COMFORTABLE TO
LOOK THROUGH SASHES WITH ODD-NUMBERED PANES
– SUCH AS A **6/6** WINDOW; A PERSON
WOULD HAVE A VIEW
THROUGH THE CENTER OF
THE WINDOW –
UNOBSTRUCTED BY A MUNTIN
(BECAUSE A **6/6** WINDOW
HAS TWO ROWS OF THREE) –
SUCH AS ONE WOULD HAVE,
FOR EXAMPLE, WITH A
2/1 WINDOW.

SASH
CONFIGURATIONS:
<u>YES:</u>
6/6, 9/9
<u>MAYBE NOT:</u>
2/1, 2/2, 4/4,
8/8, 12/12.

Consider This...

"GARDEN GROWING WILD

GROW GRASSES, MOSSES, BUSHES,
FLOWERS, AND TREES IN A WAY
WHICH COMES CLOSE TO THE WAY
THEY OCCUR IN NATURE."
A PATTERN LANGUAGE
CHRISTOPHER ALEXANDER @ 1977
P. 1073